A YEAR IN JAMAICA

Memoirs of a Girl in Arcadia in 1889

A Year in Jamaica

Memoirs of a Girl in Arcadia in 1889

DIANA LEWES

First published by Eland Publishing Ltd
61 Exmouth Market, London EC1R 4QL in 2013

ISBN 978 1 906011 83 3

Cover image: A Waiter, from a portfolio of
privately printed watercolours of the
West Indies (colour litho) by A. S. Forrest
(1869–1963)/Private Collection/The Stapleton
Collection/The Bridgeman Art Library
Digitally enhanced family photographs
© Nicholas Noble

Text set in Great Britain by Antony Gray
Printed and bound by CPI Group (UK) Ltd

Dedication

To my parents, William and Christine,
and my wife and children,
Frances, Victoria and Edward,
with all my love.

To my university tutors,
Dr David Crane and Dr Derek Todd,
to whom I am most grateful.

Contents

Foreword

I FIRST READ my great-aunt Diana Lewes's memoirs of her stay in Jamaica in 1889 in my early twenties and and was captivated by them. I always dreamed of seeing them published and finally, about forty years later, here they are. Her memoirs capture a moment in the complex social history of Jamaica in the late 1800s observed by an innocent eye. They raise and discuss difficult subjects such as sex and race without harm precisely because of this innocence. Like a colonial version of a heroine in Jane Austen, we hear this teenage Victorian trying to make sense of the complicated world the grown-ups have constructed around her, and with her we too feel the exhilaration and freedom that Jamaica offered to a girl brought up in England. Alongside her, we also try to fathom the darker currents that run through the story. I believe that these memoirs will resonate with anyone who, like me, has spent their childhood in Jamaica or indeed anyone else who has fallen under the island's spell. Although she returns to England, Diana took with her from Jamaica something which remained with her for the rest of her life.

Diana's family involvement in Jamaica began when her grandfather, William Sewell, emigrated there shortly after the abolition of slavery in 1833. Many estate owners at that time thought that sugar plantations would be uneconomic without slave labour. For example, Elizabeth Barrett Browning, whose father owned land in Jamaica, wrote on 27 May 1833 that 'the West Indies are irreparably ruined if the bill [ie the Act for the Abolition of Slavery] passes'. In this environment, William Sewell and his partner, Simon Thomson, bought many estates at knockdown prices. A number of these were estates previously owned by the Barrett family, including Oxford, which features prominently in this book. Simon went on to marry William's daughter, Lizzie. When he died childless, William inherited the share of the estates which he did not already own, making him a very wealthy man. Before he died in 1872, he realised that his son, Henry Sewell, was a spendthrift and left his estates in trust for his grandchildren (Diana and her siblings) with Henry as trustee. Henry's extravagance, and his ambiguous alliance with his attorney, Herr Bauer, make up one of the many intriguing strands in these memoirs.

The family connection with Jamaica continued into the 1960s and '70s, when all the estates were finally sold. My mother, who knew Arcadia in the 1950s and '60s writes:

> There was a magic about Arcadia. It was a gem in a beautiful situation on a high ridge overlooking the sea with the approach though handsome gates and an avenue of royal palms. It was a striking entrance. The house was square with walls made of cut stone and the beautiful verandahs had wrought-iron balustrades. The peacocks always reigned supreme in the gardens and common around the house with their magnificent tails either trailing after them or erected. But their early morning calls were very raucous.

Diana's niece (Beattie's daughter), Isabel Whitney, wrote of her visit in 1930:

> Jamaica was always at the back of my brother's and my

consciousness growing up, another world, yet always part of our family. Perhaps it was talked about, I don't remember. Some knowledge of our family connections must have seeped into our minds, children seem to be expected to know all the details relating to their forebears, but of course they don't because people never tell them anything that makes connections, only isolated stories, and their parents' conversations are references to events long past.

The year 1930 was not only my first visit to Jamaica, it was also a visit to the past, to the turn of the century when my grandmother's rule had put a stamp on the house I was about to enter and live in for two months.

I crossed the threshold of Arcadia and found myself in 1903, the year my mother had left her Jamaican home for a different life. There is a poem by the French poet, Paul Verlaine, that expresses the feeling I experienced. A rough translation of it reads:

Having pushed open the narrow, creaking door,
I found myself walking in the little garden ...
Nothing had changed.
I saw everything as it once had been.

On the ground floor I passed through the rooms that had once been the home of my great-grandparents, William and Mary, in the 1860s. William's good management and frugality had brought prosperity to his estates and he had made of Arcadia (built in 1832) a comfortable, though fairly modest, Jamaican home. The original Arcadia had been built a little further to the east along the ridge that ran 800 feet above sea level and looked down on cane fields and, beyond them, the blue Caribbean. This was the Arcadia where Lady

Nugent stayed, as recorded in her diary, and quoted on page 16. [Lady Nugent was the wife of General Sir George Nugent, who was Lieutenant Governor of Jamaica from 27 July 1801 to 20 February 1806. She stayed at the original Arcadia on a tour of Jamaica with her husband on 31 March and 1 April 1802.]

Isabel would probably have been welcomed on the front steps of Arcadia by her Uncle Philip, with his pipe and dog, looking much as he does in the photograph facing page 217. For now, however, it is his sister who introduces us to their Jamaican world in 1889.

Nicholas Noble

2013

A Very Short Glossary

Buckra	a white man
Busha	title given to manager or overseer on a sugar plantation, hence
Busha House	manager or overseer's house on a plantation
Cho-Cho	a tropical vegetable, the chayote, with a bland taste
Pic'ny/Piccaninny	a black child
Obeah	folk magic, sorcery and religious practices derived from West Africa, specifically the Igbo tribe
Peenies	fireflies

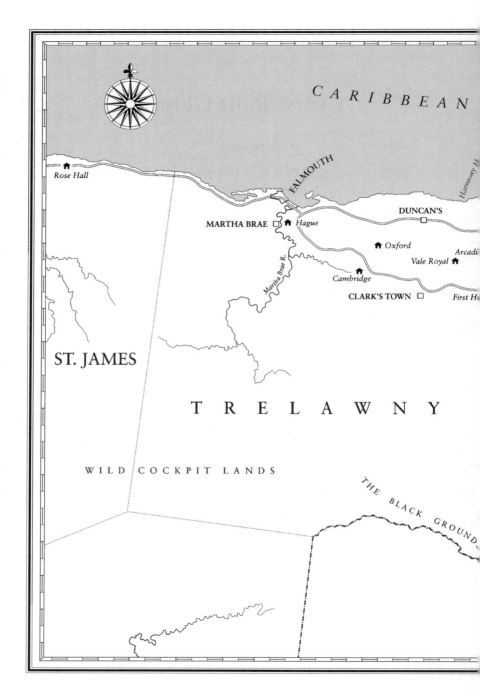

CARIBBEAN

Rose Hall

FALMOUTH

Harmony H.

MARTHA BRAE Hague

DUNCAN'S

Oxford

Vale Royal Arcadi

Cambridge

CLARK'S TOWN First H.

Martha Brae R.

ST. JAMES

TRELAWNY

WILD COCKPIT LANDS

THE BLACK GROUND

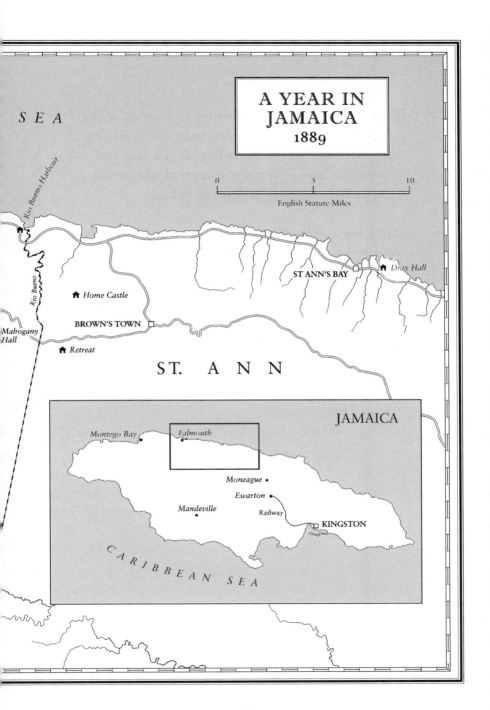

SEA

Rio Bueno Harbour

Rio Bueno

A YEAR IN
JAMAICA
1889

0   5   10

English Statute Miles

ST ANN'S BAY   ♠ Drax Hall

♠ Home Castle

BROWN'S TOWN

Mahogany
Hall

♠ Retreat

ST. ANN

JAMAICA

Montego Bay   Falmouth

Moneague ▪

Ewarton ▪

Mandeville   Railway   □ KINGSTON
▪

CARIBBEAN SEA

March 31st 1802 ... we proceeded to Arcadia, where we arrived at 6. Found a party ready to receive us, and sat down to dinner before 7. To bed early. Everything here is so quiet, clean and comfortable, that we feel ourselves in Arcadia indeed.

April 1st ... This house is not large, but it is very neat and convenient. It stands on a high hill, overlooking the sea and a great extent of beautiful country.

From *Lady Nugent's Journal*

CHAPTER 1

Arcadia

IN THE YEAR 1889, when I was sixteen and my sister
Beattie four years older, we were taken by our parents
from our home in England to Jamaica where my father
owned a number of properties and a house at Arcadia.
This he regarded as his home.

My father was a compact, dignified looking man. He
had a determined face and round blue eyes set wide apart.
In character he was self-willed and took immediate and
effective action to suppress any opposition to his wishes.
People who came to his house had either to agree with him
or to resign themselves to the knowledge that they would
no longer be welcomed. In England I had not really noticed
this characteristic. There he had been the ideal father
made up of qualities which I had considered as being
proper to all dear and beloved parents. At meals he had
sat at the other end of the table from my mother and had
fulfilled all the functions which I had imagined fathers
should fulfil. He had not conformed with my slowly built
up ideal in two ways alone: he had always got up late and
he had never written any letters.

When I had stayed with my friends in their homes and
noticed that their fathers braved the noise and confusion of
a family breakfast, a feeling of surprise and insecurity
took hold of me. It seemed for a moment possible that my
father, in differing from other fathers, differed from my
conception of what he was. My mother, on the other hand,

gave me no such cause for anxiety and remained to the end true to my picture of her. I now know that, had I remained in England, I would never have learnt to understand my father or his point of view. He would have remained cloaked for all time by my mother who, in her relations with her large family, always referred back to him for authority.

*   *   *

Arcadia house was surrounded by a wide verandah. The rooms were lofty and spacious. Those on the first floor opened outwards on to the verandah and inwards on to the upper landing. There is little privacy in a tropical house. Small sounds can be easily heard anywhere. My sister and I found ourselves thrown into close companionship with two people whom we loved but who were in many ways strangers to us.

Looking back on those days, Beattie and I would usually, after an early morning walk and breakfast, settle down on the shady side of the verandah and, taking it in turns, read aloud or sew until it was cool enough to ride. Lunch, in the middle of the day, would come as an unwelcome inter-ruption. We read Gibbon's *Decline and Fall* in this way from cover to cover and I think it had a greater influence on me than any other book I read at that time. I had nothing to compare with those far-off occurrences. The difference in period and morals meant nothing to me and, as I munched yam and sweet potatoes abstractedly, I felt that, had I like the author been given the gift of under-standing, I would have liked to divine the causes which actuated human beings around me to behave as they did.

Every morning at eleven o'clock Henry, the black coach-man, would drive the single buggy round to the front door to take my father to the office. I knew that my father owned a number of estates, possessing such names as Arcadia, Vale Royal, Drax Hall, Oxford and Cambridge, but I found it hard to visualise a man who never wrote any letters in an office. It was perhaps possible that, in his office, he was transformed into a different person and that the contemplation of such things as rum, stock and land values changed him into an active businessman, but such a metamorphosis did not seem likely. My curiosity must have become apparent for one day he invited me to go with him. That morning the double buggy came round and I climbed in feeling that a mystery was about to be elucidated.

We drove for about three miles. Once he ordered Henry to pull up by a cane field and made some remark on the growth of the canes. Later he said, 'It's dry, we want rain for the tops.' These interjections and Henry's answer 'Yes Massa, berry dry,' were in keeping with what I imagined for my new business father and, preoccupied with my own thoughts, I made no answer when he suggested good-humouredly that I should learn the names of all the cane pieces.

When he reached the office he got out, telling me to wait where I was. He walked up the flight of stone steps and disappeared into an open doorway. Henry did not un-harness the horses but let them stand in the shade of a tree and I suppose they were used to this for they remained quiet. Then Henry, like my father, went away. He was lame and walked stiffly. I was left alone with my thoughts. The estate sugar works, boiler house and trash houses were below me. The estate was 'about' and the yard was full of busy black men and women who were carrying canes to the mill. The hum of the big engine and the voices of the workers came up to me on the hot air; one of the men was singing and the others swelled the refrain.

Presently Herr Bauer, my father's attorney, came down

the steps and asked me if I would like to see the office. He was a big fair man with unusually long arms and legs, a florid complexion and a thick-growing red beard. He was German by birth and had emigrated to Jamaica. In response to this invitation, I followed him obediently and peeped into the room from which he had descended and, as I had expected, I saw the desks, the high stool and the ledgers. Once in the room, I found it difficult to breathe. My father was leaning against a desk at the far end of the room. He paid no attention to me and, in fact, I don't think he saw me. Another younger man slipped off a stool and came and shook hands. He was, I afterwards learned, the clerk and a kindly man. Herr Bauer paid no further attention to me as I hesitated at the entrance to the room but continued with a conversation which had evidently begun before I came in and which he had interrupted in order to fetch me. He spoke in a loud voice. It seemed to me strange that he should have invited me into the office only to ignore me once I was there and I stiffened as if in response to some unknown danger. This awkward situation lasted some minutes until finally my father raised his head and finally saw me. His voice when he addressed me was, for him, unusually gentle but all he said was, 'You can go back to the buggy,' and I went.

During that winter we spent in Jamaica, our mother often took us to an estate in the hills to watch polo matches. There we made friends among the polo players and these young men, some of whom lived fifty or more miles away, fell into the habit of coming to us for tennis on Saturdays. The intervening afternoons were filled with long rides during which we explored the countryside around Arcadia or with bathes in the turquoise sea at Harmony Hall Wharf. This pleasant life continued for two or three months until one day my father announced that he was going back to England, that our home there was to be sold, and that we were to remain in Jamaica with our mother. The news came as a shock to us for we had looked on our stay in Jamaica as a more or less pleasant interlude; and, now that it was prolonged indefinitely, our holiday began to assume more the proportions of a banishment from all we held dear.

My father drove away one lovely morning soon afterwards, leaving in a buggy drawn by two thoroughbred horses. Our farewells were, no doubt, lacking in warmth but our manners were submissive and our parting words correct. We heard the following Saturday that he had, on his way across the island, called at the polo club and forbidden our friends to come to tennis until he returned from England. Why my father did this I did not know and why he chose to let us hear of his wishes through others remained a mystery. His secrecy, in any event, hurt us more than his arbitrary action. After a last glorious tennis party, my mother, my sister and I settled down to solitude in the big house. Outwardly everything went on much as usual. My mother, though she said nothing to us about it, quite obviously disagreed with this action of my father's. My father, on the other hand, must have thought that he was justified. Walking to and fro on the verandah a thousand feet above the Caribbean Sea discussing this, Beattie and I felt that we had done nothing to have merited this second blow.

I may have given the impression that my father was a hard man, hard at any rate to his children, but this was not the case. Friends often said to me, 'What a delightful man your father is, I wish he were mine.' And, up to a certain point, they were right. He was a delightful man and, when he wished, he could charm anyone. On the ship out to Jamaica, for instance, I had noticed that he was the favourite after-dinner speaker and was sought after by all. But to charm others requires effort and few people are ready and willing to charm their own children. My father was probably a lazy man but he was at least brilliant. When an effort was necessary and seemed to him to be worthwhile, he was capable of making it. He normally entertained at either lunch or dinner for on these occasions he found conviviality – wine and good food – bridged the constraint which came with strangers. I suppose it was unreasonable to expect such a man to pay court to his children. He knew no other way to attract than through the charm of words or manner which, for him, entailed both physical and mental exertion. Many times we bored him except, for example, when we amused him by repeating items of news we had gleaned. I was quick to realise this and for a time made fun of our few neighbours. But the day came when he snubbed me. Perhaps I chose my moment badly or perhaps he was feeling irritable at the time. In any case I took his rebuff to heart and stopped being amusing at other people's expense. Therefore it fell out that there were many days when he neither talked to us nor wished for us to talk to him or among ourselves.

We admired our father and expressed our admiration by calling him suave which was the only word that seemed to proclaim and explain what he was. He could, when he was willing to exert himself, charm anybody and, at the same time, he could be very different when he chose to be, showing annoyance without losing his dignity or in any way disturbing himself. He was a strong man and we were not able to forget him so that, even during the months he was in England, his personality filled the house and we would not have been surprised if, at some moment, he had stepped out of the darkness of one of the doors to meet us.

CHAPTER 2

Mahogany Hall

W HILE MY FATHER WAS AWAY in England, one day was very much like another. Each morning we got up early and took a short walk while it was still cool. At seven we drank tea on the verandah; at nine we bathed and dressed for the day; at ten breakfast was served; at one lunch; and at seven thirty dinner. Looking back, those days seemed to be little more than a procession of meals which were served with the same ceremony as if my father was still at home. Punctually to the minute, Jack, our black butler, rang the bell and bowed us into the dining room. Behind the door stood Albert, the 'boy'. He, like Jack, was dressed in white; his hands were encased in cotton gloves and his face was as glossy as soap and water could make it.

Until Jack, his superior, entered with the first dish and gave him a sign to follow with the vegetables, Albert stood there, his hands clasped behind his back, immovable but for his eyes which roved from side to side, resting now on a dish which he might have placed amiss, now on a fork or a spoon a little askew. As a rule, Jack and Albert waited silently but there were days when things went wrong. Perhaps Jack thought that Albert had presumed too much in handing around a special plate. Then we would hear a slap administered with the open palm on starched linen and we trembled for the dish which was snatched from us and again presented at a different level. After these scuffles, Albert retreated once more to his place behind the door and only occasionally did I catch the glint of white when the light caught his roving eye.

Of course other things happened as well as the meals. In the morning, we read or sewed and, in the afternoon, we rode, but nothing broke the monotony; the days formed themselves into a procession of meals and the weeks into a long chain of Sundays when we drove to church in our English clothes and joined in the hymns and listened to the sermon. At first these visits to church amused me. The black women in front, who had stopped at the gate to put on their shoes, knelt with their elbows on their seats and, when I happened to look up unexpectedly, I met a row of dark eyes gazing solemnly at me over the back of their pew. The reason for this transpired later when a whole family appeared in exact copies of my and my sister's dresses. Once even a hen and chickens walked in at the open door of the church and proceeded up the aisle. In the end, however, one sermon seemed to fuse in my mind with another until I woke wondering if the Rector had said this or that on the previous Sunday or the Sunday before or if he had begun that morning with the Sermon on the Mount and carried us uninterrupted through the whole Gospel of Saint Luke. Coming home, Henry raced and overtook every buggy which had left the church gate before us while my mother, apparently unconscious of the speed at which we were travelling, chatted calmly to my sister in the back of the carriage.

There were days when my mother said to us: 'Why don't you ride over to Mahogany Hall and see Lucy and Catherine?'

I loved those days. It was nine miles to Mahogany Hall, and we had to get off in good time.

There were several reasons why those expeditions were

particularly lovely. The days were nearly always fine with the sun shining and the wind blowing. I don't know if my mother had any special foresight about the weather but it generally turned out that she had seen far enough ahead to send a note by post boy the previous day to announce our arrival to Lucy and Catherine. By two o'clock we would be mounted and on our way.

Our route took us inland towards the hills. We left the sugar works and cane fields behind us and followed a rough estates road through the hills and the logwood groves. Where the land was level, we cantered but, for the greater part of the way, it was too rough for quick riding. After about six miles of this sort of going, we reached the main road and pulled up in the shade of a big tree to cool our mounts, which showed dark streaks of sweat on their glossy coats. While we waited, a buggy came trotting by with dusty-looking men and women and a string of donkeys with laden panniers came into view. The jolly black women who followed them greeted us with shouts of 'Evenin' Misses. Evenin' me darlin' buckra Misses.'

The main road had something different about it from other roads I knew. It had a joke connected with it and it was as if I expected to see the joke come to life and go sidling into the sunny distance. Once one of our friends had driven a newcomer through that part of the island and, as they came to the last bend after leaving Clark's Town, and they saw that mile-long stretch of road before them, the newcomer had exclaimed, 'What a straight road!' and our friend had replied, 'Yes, Roman of course.' The newcomer was supposed to have made the answer, 'Dear me, yes. Wonderful roads those old johnnies constructed.' That was the joke which I saw and which even now I see when I think of that road near Clark's Town.

But, by the time my thoughts reached this point, my sister had moved out from the shade left by the tree into the sunshine and I followed her through Clark's Town and up First Hill where the bananas and coconut trees grew so thickly that it was dark and shady. From First Hill it was not far to Mahogany Hall but, as the district is appropriately named and First Hill is the first of many hills, the time it takes to traverse that stretch of road is considerable. A buggy and two horses could fly down the steep hills but it was not so comfortable to descend them rapidly on horseback. Mahogany Hall, however, possessed the most perfect park-like common and there we made up for lost time and galloped for over a mile under huge cotton trees and round clumps of bamboo.

The Lockets were proud of their park and they would sometimes meet us on horseback at the entrance gate and join us in a race to the house. On this afternoon we were not disappointed for Lucy and Catherine were there waiting for us. They were dressed in old-fashioned riding habits buttoned from neck to waist and cut away over the hips, leaving two tails hanging down behind. Lucy was small with a round smiling face and bright eyes. I didn't know why but she always reminded me of my eldest brother, Philip, and she had the same way of putting me at my ease. She was pleasant too, fond of teasing and interested in little, everyday affairs. Catherine, on the other hand, was much taller and just as thin, but she was grave. She did not, at that time, remind me of anyone in the same way as Lucy and, although she had big, dark eyes and a straight nose and, although she was better looking than her sister, I always preferred racing with Lucy.

Tea was served in the large, dark drawing room at Mahogany Hall. The floor was constructed of dark and light woods, laid alternately, and polished to a high degree and from this the house took its name, mahogany being the wood used for the darker strips. The furniture was early Victorian, the ceiling high and lost in shadows. The doors were heavy, not a sound coming through them from the rest of the house and only an occasional breath of cool air penetrated the closely jalousied windows. This room had been built during the years when all planters were wealthy and something of the elegance and luxuriousness of those days lingered, lending it dignity and calm. I tiptoed in, feeling that my high riding boots were out of place, and sat down on a black and gold chair near the tea table.

Mrs Locket was a tall, dignified woman and wore her hair looped over her ears and coiled close to the back of her head. Mr Locket was shorter, his bushy side whiskers and thick wavy hair were white. They were old-fashioned people and ceremonious in their manners. In the house, on a limited income, they clung to the same habits of ostentation and display to which they had been accustomed in their early married life.

Often, when I had sat silent for any length of time, people seemed to ask me strange questions which threw me into a state of confusion. Inexperience and the fear that I might not meet the situation calmly – that I might not only not be able to find the correct answer to an unexpected question but that I might, in fact, find no answer correct or otherwise – worried me. I was conscious that Mr Locket was looking at me and the twinkle in his little blue eyes did not bode well.

'What is she thinking about?' he said suddenly. And his son Charles, a young man of twenty-five, who had entered the room a few minutes before and placed himself by my sister's chair, replied, 'Bundle, I suppose.'

Now Bundle was my dog and I was very fond of him but I certainly was not thinking of him at that moment. I was really wondering why Lucy reminded me of Philip, my eldest brother whom I loved, and Herr Bauer and how all three managed to be so alike and so different; and why likenesses in people did not depend on pleasantness but on something else. However, of course, I could not explain all this when I said I was not thinking of Bundle.

Mr Locket's question and Charles' ridiculous answer focused the attention of all those present on me and threw me into the state of confusion which I dreaded. Mrs Locket who, up to that moment had appeared to me to be kindly and amiable, took on an air of austerity. She, like her daughters, was buttoned from neck to waist and her satin dress glittered formidably. So upset was I that I hardly dared to lift my eyes from above the big cameo brooch pinned to her bosom.

At that moment a barefooted Jamaican girl entered with a silver teapot and a hot water jug on a tray. To reach the table, she had to pass in front of me and, meeting my glance, she interrupted her advance to bob me a curtsey. Her movement caused the hot water to shoot from the spout of the pot and drew an ejaculation of horror from her mistress.

'Christ,' said the girl complacently and, putting down her burden on the table, she produced a cloth from somewhere about her person and flung it on the floor where the water had already dimmed the brilliance of the boards. Her clumsy action completely upset the ceremony of the occasion and restored me to my self-possession.

While Mr Locket and his son muttered such observations as 'Blast the girl,' the young girl placed her feet on the cloth and shuffled to and fro until she had removed the water, but not the stain, from the floor. By her manner she showed me that she was used to such epithets and indifferent to them for, while her feet moved rapidly to and fro, she continued to regard me earnestly.

During all this time, Lucy had not ceased to talk as if she thought, by that means, she might smooth over her mother's anger, her father's annoyance and the girl's shortcomings with which she was evidently familiar.

When the Lockets had recovered from this upset and we had been served with tea, Catherine made a suggestion. We four – Lucy, Catherine, Beattie and I – should go for a gallop together. It seemed that long shallow trenches crossed the pastures to the north of the main road (our Roman road) and that they made the most perfect obstacles to jump. These trenches had been dug to carry water off in rainy weather but, even when dry, they were, Catherine said, deep enough and wide enough to make fine jumps.

There was a pause after she had spoken. I looked at Beattie, she looked at Catherine, and then said she was doubtful if her horse would jump. I knew nothing of the capabilities of my horse, Victoria, but longed to try her and began to feel afraid that something might prevent us from going. Catherine, however, settled the matter by saying, 'All horses can jump if they have a lead.' Therefore, before we set out on our ride home, it was decided (provided mother gave us her permission) that we should meet on the following Wednesday.

We had to trot nearly all the way home. I asked Beattie why Philip, Lucy and Herr Bauer were so much alike and if she really liked Catherine better than Lucy. She answered rather shortly, 'Yes I do.' This relieved me of a responsibility because, firstly, I did not, and, secondly, I thought I might have been selfish in always galloping with Lucy.

However, the other half of my question took a great deal longer to answer. In fact it grew and developed into a conversation which lasted up and down First Hill, all through Clark's Town, and all along our by-road. When Peterkin, my stable boy, rose like a funny black and white goblin from the front steps at Arcadia and took Victoria's reins, I had just heard something about Herr Bauer that I had never known before. So, when Peterkin said, in his gentle way, 'Me berry glad to know dat Victoria go well, Missie Di,' I just gave a quick hug to Victoria and ran up the steps into the house.

When we told Mother that we had been invited to ride with the Lockets, we did not mention the jumps. Mother had a great admiration for the Lockets and always said, 'They are splendid horsewomen.' No entreaties were needed for permission to ride with them but jumps would have been a different matter. Still, as she always seemed to know what I had done or was about to do, I did not feel comfortable at this concealment. I think perhaps I should try to explain this gift of my mother's, even though it is not easy to put it into words. When I was alone with her she seemed to think as I did, to agree with what I said, to be understanding and sympathetic; but, when other people were present and we had to be social, all this altered; in some strange, inexpressible way she turned into another person. After dances or tennis parties, she would say, 'How many times did you dance with Jim?' or 'How many times did you play with Bill?' And, at times, this was awkward for it happened that the person she mentioned was exactly the one I had danced or played with most. Because of all this I had fallen into the habit of telling her everything without waiting to be asked. Beattie, on the other hand, could hide anything without appearing to do so and it was she who said when we sat down for dinner that evening, 'The Lockets have asked us to ride with them,' supplementing her remark with a kick under the table to keep me quiet.

As usual Jack carried two of the tall silver candlesticks up to the verandah after dinner and placed them on the round iron table at the south-west corner of the house. These candles were covered by glass shades and were thus protected from the land breeze which crept down from the hills about an hour after sunset, bringing with it all sorts of pleasant smells. The shades completely protected the candles from the breeze but not from the large, fluffy moths which, every now and then, flew in attracted by the light.

On this particular evening, Beattie and I settled ourselves in the rocking chairs with our books. After we had been reading for some time, one of these moths flew in, swift and big as a bird, and began to batter against first one and then another of the shades. I had often seen moths do this in the schoolroom at home in England when the lamp was lit and the windows were open. I waited for this one, with a wing span of four or five inches and a body as big as a hummingbird's, to do the same, fall in through the open top of the glass shade and burn itself. It was therefore with relief that I realised that it had disappeared as swiftly and silently into the night as it had come, leaving Mother, Beattie and me alone.

Beattie had not moved during the onslaught of the moth but Mother, who was sitting on an iron chair with her needlework spread out before her, lifted her head when it first struck the shade and remained still, her needle poised in her hand, her body tense, until it disappeared. Mother was tall and fair. She had been born and brought up on the Westmorland Fells and retained some of the vigour and energy of her youth even in the heat of the tropics. I had never known her to loll in a chair and yet she was not abrupt in her manner or managing. There was a steel-like determination in the way she set about her life but it seemed to be more a mastery over herself which she sought than control over others. Our big Jamaican house with its large staff of servants and dependants must have struck a young English girl as strange but she had taken up the reins of management with energy and, with infinite patience, she controlled and guided the servants who came to her with their troubles, their sicknesses, and their domestic anxieties. Big creole establishments were much like small courts in those days. Everything in them was done on a lavish scale. Money was not spared. All stores which were not procured locally had to be arranged for and brought over from Europe or America and these had to be thought of and ordered six months before they were required. My father hired a sailing barque which made one voyage from England and two from New York in each year. She carried sugar and rum on her outward trips and brought back machinery for the estates, stores, cutlasses, staves for barrels etc. but also everything that might be required in the big house: casks of light wines, dry goods, kegs of Danish butter, oil, soap and many other necessities and luxuries. I had gone many times with my mother, Mary the cook, Jack the butler and Henry the coachman into the store rooms and watched her give out what was required for each department. I had also often sat by her at her desk watching her making out lists and comparing catalogues and prices. Parents brought their disobedient children to the front steps with requests that the 'Big Massa' might 'see him bad chil beaten' but it was to the back verandah that the sick came. On the lower back verandah were two long fowl coops which had originally belonged to the sailing barque and had, most likely, made many voyages across the Atlantic. These now stood just outside the back door and, at all times of the day or evening, groups sat there waiting for 'Big Misses' to beg for pills, ointment or bandages. I loved to watch Mother interviewing these sufferers and to listen to her admonitions and kindly rebukes. I think she liked to do this and I know they rewarded her by devotion and implicit trust.

On this evening I did not, at once, take up my book again when the moth had flown away. My mind was only too ready to let itself be distracted, so slipping a finger into the page to keep the place, I let my mind wander back over the things that had happened during the day.

First I thought of our ride across the common at Mahogany Hall – of the cotton trees which towered over the surrounding grass, of the huge clusters of bamboo and of the banana walks set back in sheltered corners. And all the things, as I thought of them in time, seemed more real to me than they had been while I had ridden among them.

Then I thought of the people I had seen during the day and these, too, seemed clearer and more understandable now that I thought of them than when they had been talking to me. In some odd way I liked them better. Lucy was kinder, more cheerful and more practical. And this brought me back to the question I had asked Beattie on our ride home and to her answer. She had said that Philip, Lucy and Herr Bauer in his own way did try to please others: that they were all three a little conventional and that they relied on their social position to give them strength. Now, when I came to think this over, I could see that Lucy did try very hard to please me whenever we met and that she referred to her father's position more often than most other people would have done. Philip, too, spoke of himself as the future head of our family and Herr Bauer seemed to set more on his position as attorney than he did exactly on himself as a person.

Beattie had gone on to say that they all seemed able to make a social occasion of almost any meeting of one or two. They never let the conversation lapse like my father who said his say and then took for granted that that was all there was to be said; finally they were all reasonable, hard-working and energetic people.

Perhaps, had I liked all these people equally, I might have found it easier to see and understand where they resembled each other, but my dislike of Herr Bauer made it hard for me to judge him fairly. Beattie, however, found no difficulty in giving him his due and pointed out that Herr Bauer was a conscientious man and that he, like Philip, excelled in detail, liked to be liked, setting great store on what other people thought of him.

On top of these thoughts came another. I was not certain if my mother was a fourth 'pleasing' person. She puzzled me for, in some ways, she seemed to be like Lucy and in other ways like me and yet I knew there was no likeness between Lucy and myself.

That night, when I was safe in bed with the door between my sister's room and mine wide open and the sheet pulled up to my chin, Beattie told me that once, long ago, Herr Bauer had wanted to marry a friend who had stayed in our house and that this friend had refused him and married someone else. This, she said, had made Herr Bauer bitter against us. Beattie's voice was low for fear we should be overheard and so a great deal of what she said was lost in her bedclothes. But, when the solitary part of the night began to creep in through the jalousies, all this did not seem to matter very much and I fell asleep thinking I should like to be the moon.

CHAPTER 3

The Murderer

W E DID NOT MEET THE LOCKETS on the following Wednesday, nor on the Wednesday after that. In fact it was months before our ride came off. This delay had nothing to do with the discovery of our intention to jump trenches. It was caused by a quite unexpected circumstance.

Beattie and I were riding over a lonely stretch of country one afternoon. The track we were on followed the dry bed of a stream: at no place could we see more than a few yards ahead. I was cantering along swinging to right and left as the road twisted and turned with the course of the waterless gully when a man jumped out from behind a rock and frightened Victoria. He had evidently intended to catch my reins but had miscalculated the pace at which I was going and only succeeded in frightening my horse who bolted. My sister's horse, St Hilaria, following closely and confronted suddenly by a strange man, gave a jump, nearly unseating Beattie, and knocked him down.

When we pulled up and looked back, the man had disappeared. He might never have been. The track, overshadowed here and there by trees, was devoid of life and neither above on the hill side nor below in the gully could I see anyone.

'Shall I go back?' I asked, my intention being to apologise for the accident and to see if the man was any the worse for his fall.

'No,' said Beattie. 'It was his own fault,' and, since I could see that Beattie had been frightened, I said no more about going back. Little things seemed important when one had nothing much to think about, but some incidents seemed to drift out of one's mind and leave nothing behind them but a vague sense of confusion.

At dinner Jack informed us that the local police had called during the afternoon to say that a man had escaped from prison and that some people had seen a suspicious looking character in our neighbourhood. Jack was so full of this news and so puffed up with importance that he snatched the dish of yams from Albert and carried it into the hall without giving us an opportunity to help ourselves. 'Him bad man, Misses,' he said, hurrying back into the room. 'Inspector him telephone to de Barracks to say no man is to travel singly. So de Sargant and de Cahpral and de two policemen all ride up dis arternoon. Dey say dey see not'in on de road.'

I signed to Albert that I would like the yam but, although he knew what I wanted and although he looked distressed, he made no effort to get them.

Jack went in and out of the room several times bringing with him each time a more hair-raising description of the escaped prisoner. He was now a burglar, now a murderer under sentence of death. I ate the whole beef rissole in a sort of dream, tasting nothing.

Mother and Beattie looked theatrical; not as if they had forgotten their own parts in a play but as if they were afraid one of the other actors had done so. Mother spoke to Jack in a soothing voice; she had several ideas. 'Will you warn the household servants,' she said, 'and the stablemen?' Then, her thoughts wandering further afield, 'And what about the mutton woman? Doesn't she come this afternoon?'

'De mutton woman,' Jack's scorn was terrible. Evidently

37

not even an escaped prisoner would attack the mutton
woman. He was so indignant that I wanted to laugh.

'He might be hungry,' I suggested.

'But the mutton isn't cooked,' said Beattie. 'It's not
cooked until it gets ... '

Here Beattie stopped and an odd, startled look came
over her face. Her eyes were wide open and concentrated
on something that seemed to be just outside me.

'What about our man?' she said in a small voice.

'Our man! Oh! Yes.'

Of course there was the man. How strange it was that,
until Beattie spoke, I should have forgotten all about him.
The man, really, had not seemed important; his sudden
appearance had been everything, he himself nothing.

'Yes, of course there was that man,' I said feeling flat
and rather disappointed.

'What man?' said Mother, looking from Beattie to me,
then, receiving no enlightenment from me, back again to
Beattie.

The odd concentrated look had gone out of Beattie's
eyes and she had grown pink.

'A man jumped out,' she said in an embarrassed voice,
'at Victoria.'

'And missed her,' I added.

'At St Hilaria ... '

'Who knocked him down ... '

'A black man?' cried Jack, his voice trembling with
excitement.

'Yes.'

'In white cloe?'

Yes, of course, he had been white like the rock and grey
like the dust of the road which he had disturbed as he fell
and lay sprawling.

'De murderer,' shrieked Jack.

'Dear Lard,' sobbed Albert. And, as if he expected to see our assailant come to life and strike us down before his eyes, he seized up the bread knife and platter and rushed from the room.

After that, all rides were forbidden for a time and, even after the prisoner had been caught and put back in gaol, Mother insisted on our taking Peterkin or William, the under groom, with us when we went out. Peterkin was alright but William would insist on singing hymns in a loud voice; and, as his mule seemed able only to proceed at a walk or a gallop, we were continually losing him or being startled by the rapidity of his approach. Therefore we found it less trouble to give up riding and to take our exercise on the verandah.

'Are all real things disappointing?' I asked Beattie, as we walked dejectedly to and fro for the third morning in succession.

'What do you mean?' she answered crossly.

She was annoyed because Mother had suggested that, as we spent so much time on the verandah, we might disentangle the stephanotis which grew luxuriantly on the iron railings and supports and put it up again tidily.

'Well,' I began in an endeavour to explain, 'if that man really intended to murder us why wasn't it more exciting? I could have imagined something a great deal better myself.'

'I dare say you could have,' said Beattie sourly, 'but it would not have been the same. Real things are like that ... tiresome,' and she tugged a large piece of stephanotis out of the railing.

Her tone of voice, even more than her words, made everything hopeless and I sat down on a long tendril which I had uncoiled and looked at her reproachfully. It was hard

enough trying to fit oneself into a life full of practical details
continually eluding one without having to suffer this final
difficulty, a misunderstanding with one's best friend.

'Do you think we have done enough and that I can let
this piece curl up again?' I asked presently.

'I hate useless occupations and things that make my
hands a mess,' Beattie replied.

'Well, then, let's think of people,' I suggested more hope-
fully and soon we were deep in the one subject which never
bored us, a subject as involved as the stephanotis tendrils
and as difficult to disentangle but which never failed to
interest us and which seemed to carry us along a road
which might lead somewhere.

We had decided about our father being 'suave' and
Philip, Lucy and Herr Bauer being 'pleasing' and I asked
her if she thought there were many other sorts of
characters. She said at once that there were the people
like George and people like May's father.

George was the first friend my eldest brother Philip
had brought home with him from Oxford. He had caused
a sort of revolution in our midst and an upheaval in our
way of life. He was slight and fair in appearance and
gentle in manner. He had spent hours playing ball over a
garden seat on the front lawn of our home in England
teaching us to return volleys and to hold our racquets
correctly. When the weather was bad, chess in the library
took the place of ball on the lawn. When Philip told us
that he played tennis for his college and that he would
probably take a first in history, we replied loyally, 'Of
course.' Nothing seemed impossible for our hero. Later,
by introducing dry batteries, he electrified the whole of
the upper floor of the house; not only did bells ring where
bells had never rung before but lights twinkled and sparks

sprang miraculously from metal bedsteads and picture rails. I don't know of how much of all this my parents were aware but I do know that we worshipped him. He brought a name with him from college for studiousness and he belonged to an old and aristocratic family, so, I suppose, they took him on trust and asked no questions.

Bill, one of our polo playing friends in Jamaica, reminded us of George and, at first, before we came to like Bill for himself, it was for his likeness to this first friend that we took to him. Bill did not take an interest in electricity or in other kindred sciences, but he studied irrigation and understood natural phenomena. He could tell us about the habits of tropical birds and animals and amuse us for hours with stories of Jamaicans. The way he looked on life and the originality he brought to bear on everyday affairs was the same as George's so, immediately Beattie mentioned George, I replied, 'Yes and Bill too.'

'What is the word which best describes those people?' I asked quickly. Remembrance of our life in England had to some extent obliterated all thought of present boredom. I was once more keen and interested.

'Simple, I think,' said Beattie.

'Why simple?'

'Because they are natural and unsocial.'

'Then why not call them natural?'

'Because all people are natural in their own way. That word wouldn't be distinctive enough. But none of the others is simple.'

'Very well,' I said, further argument seeming a waste of time, 'and May's father? What would you call him?'

'I don't know. What do you think?'

Beattie stopped and, leaning her elbows on the railings, looked out over the lawn to the sea which lay one thousand feet below us. The air was hot and the wind high. I screwed up my eyes to protect them against the glare.

'What about animal?' I said presently. 'Would that do?'

May's father was a real Englishman. He was a man one would turn to in a difficulty but not one to whom one would turn lightly or carelessly for he would know at once the right action to take. He would single out the honourable course to follow from among a host of possibilities. He was a man for whom the world contained but two sides to every question, one right and the other wrong. There may have been something a little limited in this singleness of mind, but there was something reassuring and restful in it too. May's father had been a Master of Hounds. He had led a straightforward, honourable life. He had married young and brought up a large family and ruled his household and servants. I don't believe that, with the exception of sporting books or farm periodicals, he read anything but, in his own subjects, he was a master.

'Yes that will do,' Beattie said. 'Suave, pleasing, simple and animal, those words set them out alright.'

These four characters seemed each to be complete. They contained only qualities which fitted comfortably one into another; qualities which anyone might reasonably expect to find housed in the same body. Their discovery did not surprise me but it made me feel secure. They seemed to be, in themselves, an answer which held out hope for some comprehension of all the mysteries and surprises which crowded around us.

CHAPTER 4

Mr Biggar

FOR A DAY OR TWO we were satisfied with the discovery of the four characters. 'So far so good,' I said to myself, and something of the same sort I wove into my prayers twice daily; I felt secure and announced my security triumphantly to God. However, between that first and the succeeding nights, a change set in; I began to doubt. So far all was good; but I could not feel certain of others. For instance, what about myself?

It was when I, in my thoughts, had reached this point that complete doubt took possession of my mind. Another circumstance which made things especially difficult for us was that Mother, at this particular moment, came to the conclusion (which was never far from her mind) that idleness was bad for the young. She suggested that Beattie should tidy the five big and two little drawers in her chest. Mine required less attention because I never kept more than the minimum of underclothes in daily use and squeezed all the others into the largest drawer at the bottom which was seldom opened and so never disturbed. But, in spite of this, I was scolded and told to bring another set to change into. When I had laid these ready over the back of a chair, I tidied my sponge and washing things and then fidgeted in and out watching Beattie, who was sitting on the floor in the next room, surrounded by a high tide of clothes and wondered how annoyed she would be by the time she had reduced them to order.

43

When Mother came back to see how we were getting on, she caught me half in and half out of my room, standing on one leg and one hand, my legs outside on the verandah and my head under the washstand. I was trying to see if I could retrieve the soap which had eluded me without getting into the room and was enjoying the acrobatic feat I had set myself.

I could not see my mother's face but there was an ominous restraint in the shape of her back. I made some pretext to turn, hoping to divine her mood, and collapsed on the floor.

She made no comment on the strange position in which she had found me but told me to go down to the linen cupboard and bring up a sheet which I should find there ready to be hemmed sides to middle. I walked downstairs soberly enough for I knew that I should get no sympathy from Beattie and also that Mother would not relent until the task she had set me was completed. Having found the sheet – a double one fine as gossamer with long wear and delightfully scented with dried rose leaves – I hopped all the way upstairs with it in a desperate attempt to reduce some of my excess spirits and to enjoy one last fling before settling down.

That hop was indeed my last one for some time. For two days I hemmed furiously, trying meanwhile not to think or speak or be anything but an automaton with flying fingers and a hot sticky needle. Beattie was soon put to work on the other end of the seam and the only fun I got out of it was when she and I met in the middle and fought for the last inch of material.

When the sheet was at last finished, neatly folded and put back in the linen cupboard, it was evening and I was tired. We slipped round to the north side of the verandah and stood silently looking down over the darkening sea. Behind us the long windows were barred and shuttered for the night and before us lay a mass of shadows, indifferent and uncertain in outline.

'Beattie,' I whispered, 'what character are you?' And, as she did not answer at once, I added, 'What character am I?'

The second part of my question was almost inaudible for I had become afraid. Sometimes I felt sure of myself and at other times I did not. At times I felt as if I was a complete person and then, again, without any warning I became an entirely different character with other opinions and wishes and, worst of all, different feelings. I felt that if this were true and I contained all sorts of contradictions, if I could be bold at one moment and shy at the next, if I could be delighted at the thought of a party one day and terrified in case I should have to face strangers the next, and if I were happy without a definite cause and unhappy for the same reason, how could I then be sure what I was? And, considering that I was unable to comprehend myself, how could I hope that anyone else could do so? And, as I waited for Beattie to answer, I felt as if I wanted to run away and hide.

Then, calmly, as if she had been debating a question of history, Beattie said, 'There must be people who have part of one character and part of another. They must be combined. That would account for the contradictions in them.'

'Then what do you think I am?'

'Simple and suave,' she answered, 'for you are definitely simple and then there are times when you are quite different.'

'And then you are combined too,' I said. 'Suave like

Father and pleasing like Philip,' and, upon saying this, I danced to the other end of the verandah, leaving Beattie staring after me.

'Come back here,' she called softly. 'There are still many things to work out.' And she was right. Moreover, having got as far as we had in the formation of our theory, it seemed a good idea to find someone who could give us advice on what we had done.

I had already, some days before, written out the first four characters and laid them under the handkerchiefs in my little top drawer; now, following Beattie into my room, I pulled out the carefully written sheets and handed them to her. These we decided to send, together with the two characters we had just discovered, to Mr Biggar and, with this purpose in mind, Beattie told me to go downstairs to get the pen and ink, a sheet of notepaper and an envelope.

Mother was entertaining two friends on the front porch. Had Beattie and I still not been in disgrace, we should have been invited to join them. Instead tea had been sent up to us on a tray. I slipped through the long downstairs bedroom and entered the library through the side door. I could hear high voices sifting through the house and occasional subdued bursts of laughter. In the library it was almost dark. The windows were grey squares, aloof and uninviting, the furniture was withdrawn. The only light shone in a bright band from the porch to the back hall. In the dining room, Jack was moving from the sideboard to the water cooler behind the screen. He was preparing lime drinks for dinner.

Quickly I took the things I required from the desk and, gathering them in my arms, I pressed them tightly to my chest. In some odd, intangible way I felt that this decision, which I was called on to make, was important and that I must, before I stepped out, make an effort to see where I was going. Alone in that shadowy room, I let my thoughts go back to the first and only time I had met Mr Biggar.

Mr Biggar and his pupil, Mr Costessey, had voyaged out from England with us but, as they had both been bad sailors, Beattie and I had seen nothing of them on board ship. I suppose my mother and father had, however, seen enough of Mr Biggar to like him for, after we had been at Arcadia for a few weeks, Mother said that they were coming to stay with us. She mentioned that Mr Biggar was a literary critic with the *Spectator*.

All visitors were welcome in so lonely a place as Arcadia, so even though my memory of the two travellers was vague, it being limited to two names on a passenger list and two figures in a crowded customs house, I ran downstairs pleased and excited when I heard their buggy come round the corner of the house.

Mr Biggar, who was already standing in the porch, was tall and thin. When I held my hand out to him he looked down at me with a tired expression on his face as if he had, years and years ago, weighed people like me and found us wanting. His eyes were large but terribly distant and he had a habit of opening them and screwing them up for no apparent reason. They shut me out from all communication with him, making me feel insignificant. In the hope of receiving a warmer greeting, I turned to Mr Costessey, but here again I was disappointed. Mr Costessey was shorter than Mr Biggar, shorter even than I was. He was fair and sunburnt, his mouth was sulky and he looked disconsolate. Together they made me feel awkward.

I sat down but, in my confusion, I forgot to ask them to be seated too and, for a minute or two, they remained standing, staring out of the side windows where nothing much could be seen. I noticed nothing about them but their English shoes, socks and trousers. I dared not look higher than their knees. A desultory conversation between my father and Mr Biggar continued over my head. Then Jack bowed himself in and led our visitors to their rooms. Their shoes and socks had made me feel a long way from England and home.

During the whole forty-eight hours of their visit, I never recovered from those first crushing few minutes. There was nothing friendly about the two men and nothing natural in their conversation. Mr Biggar discussed politics with my father. Mr Costessey said nothing. He was not interested in walking, swimming or riding. When Mother, Beattie and I drove to church the next morning, we left them standing on the front steps and, when we drove back after an exhilarating chase of three buggies on the road, they met us on the same spot with a travesty of welcome.

At lunch I tried to drag more than monosyllables from Mr Costessey.

'Do you like reading?' I asked breathlessly.

'No,' he replied.

'Do you come from Scotland?'

'Yes.'

'What part?'

'Banff.'

'Is that on the east coast?'

'Yes.'

'I know the Crinnan Canal and the Caledonian Canal and ... ' There I stopped; Mr Costessey was not interested. Scotland was no good. In a final effort, I hurled my last question at him. He should, I thought, be forced to give a more comprehensive opinion on a subject nearer home.

'What do you think of Jamaica?' I asked and waited anxiously for his answer. A mental upheaval was visible on his face, a blank look came into his eyes. He grew pinker than ever and, for a moment, interrupted the even transport of food from his plate to his mouth. Was I going to be rewarded?

'Well, I don't know,' he said at last and, focusing his eyes once more on his plate, he relapsed into silence.

After the first evening, when we sat for two hours in a long row on the verandah rocking ourselves to and fro in the darkness, Mother spoke to me seriously.

'You must try to be pleasant to your guests,' she said chidingly.

'I have tried,' I replied almost in tears from chagrin and disappointment.

On the second evening, I gave up all hope and, aided by the dark, I plunged into the relation of one fairy story after another. The even roll of our rockers and the voices at the far end of the row were all I could hear; soon this too ceased. I was in another world. How long my stories had gone on, I don't know. Suddenly I stopped. Complete silence had fallen on the row of chairs and on their occupants. They neither rocked nor spoke. The big stars shone over the sea and the hill breeze crept noiselessly round the end of the house. How long this silence had lasted I did not know. I felt as if I had inadvertently given myself away to a hostile audience.

Presently Mother rose and we trooped after her into the light. There we began the usual ritual of 'good-nights'. Mother ushered us in. Mr Biggar opened the door onto the upstairs landing and stood aside to let us pass. I remember that I would willingly have avoided him had that been possible for, after all, he was the cause of my confusion. As

I put out my hand I glanced up into his face and was surprised to find his eyes fixed on me.

'May I congratulate you on your daughter's talent for storytelling,' he said to my mother in his clipped, polished manner and so he dismissed me.

Here my recollection ended. Mother's friends were preparing to leave. Jack came hurrying out of the dining room. In the library, it was so quiet that I could hear the Petrea blossoms, which had been blown in through the open windows, scrape as they twisted on the polished floor.

The next morning the four first characters, suave, pleasing, simple and animal, with the two combined, suave-pleasing and simple-suave, were posted to Mr Biggar. I also put a short note into the envelope asking him if he would kindly criticise our work. This done we waited.

The two following weeks passed slowly. The interest, the life of each day centred round the arrival of the post-boy and each day grew weary and died at about eleven o'clock when the bag was opened by Jack on the back verandah. For, although one or two letters came addressed to Beattie and me, they were none of them the one we were hoping for.

Then the mail from England came in, bringing news from my father, and at once the whole household was thrown into excitement. He wrote to say that he had shut up our home in Dorset and not sold it as he had intended to do and that he was sailing to Jamaica at once, bringing Philip, my eldest brother, with him. My other brothers were to remain in England and spend their holidays in Torquay.

Upon receipt of this message, the house was spring cleaned, new horses were ordered from the hill estates and exercised by Henry in the big buggy and neighbours called to enquire about the date of their arrival. Of course Beattie and I still watched for the post-boy but not so eagerly as we had done at first and, in my heart, I began to fear that Mr Biggar was not going to reply.

Eventually the day came when our father was expected. For the last time, Beattie and I slipped up onto the verandah for a walk and discussion. In a few hours other people would be in the house; the long quiet time was nearly over.

I felt listless and disappointed. It was not in this way that I had imagined the end of one period and the beginning of another.

'Mr Biggar is not going to answer,' I said discontentedly.

'I don't know,' Beattie replied. 'He may yet.'

'It's a month since we sent off our theory.'

'It may be two months before we hear. We can only wait.'

'Then do you think he will write?' I asked.

'Yes.'

Beattie's certainty comforted me, but I was not ready to admit that I thought as she did and said, 'And if he never does?'

'He will.'

CHAPTER 5

The Cattle Count

W E WERE ON THE FRONT STEPS dressed in clean, starched dresses when my father returned from England. Henry drove furiously round the house and drew up with a flourish. Jack and Albert precipitated themselves down the steps and dragged the small luggage out of the carriage. Peter, the gardener, waited on the downstairs verandah behind the iron gate and, in the background, all the female servants were grouped. It reminded me of the day on which we, ourselves, had arrived from England. Only this time, Mother, Beattie and I were part of the reception. We were now one with Jamaica, unconsciously assimilated into a sort of feudal system.

My father got out of the buggy, kissed us and said it was nice to be back. Philip also kissed us and said we were sunburnt. He was tall and very fair and I suppose, compared with girls in England and after several months in Jamaica, we were burnt. I longed to ask him if he liked Jamaica but, as he was coming out to learn sugar planting and to settle, it seemed best to say nothing yet. Life among grown-ups had taught me that questions can be awkward and that, with a little patience, one can learn all that one wants to know without rushing into danger or courting rebuff. Philip might have been sorry to leave England, novelty might not compensate him for all he had left behind and he certainly could not yet have acquired any new interests.

The conversation was initially general and very pleasant.

I took little part in it. Except for smiling continually at first my father and then my brother I did nothing. These two nice-looking men are, I thought, my own people who have come back into my life. They must know, without any words of mine, how pleased I am to see them and how comforting it is to me to feel that they cannot be torn unexpectedly out of my life again. When Jack came to say that the hot water was ready for the travellers, I sat on by myself, staring at nothing in particular, thinking how lucky I was to have relations round me and how happy I was.

The next morning the double buggy came round after breakfast and our two men drove away to the office. I wondered what Philip would think of that horrible place. When they came back to lunch I looked at my brother, earnestly half afraid of what I might see and yet impelled to search for a change in him which I dreaded to find. As far as I could see his face showed no emotion of any sort but he seemed to have withdrawn inside himself and to be shut away. After all, I thought, this may not be altogether a bad sign. Men had more to compare new experiences with than girls had. Philip, who had spent four years at Oxford and eaten law dinners in London, must be better able than I to sum up our attorney's character. All the same, in spite of these thoughts, I made up my mind to tell my brother what I felt as soon as I had the opportunity. Herr Bauer had not come near us during my father's absence and he had, in a way, sunk into the background of my life. It was only when I watched Philip and thought of him taking up a post as apprentice under such a man that I felt anxious. Days passed quickly. More and more people came to the house. My father drove from place to place behind his young thoroughbred horses inspecting new plantations and counting stock. His trip to England had given him energy. He had come back with renewed interest in his large properties and hope of better and more prosperous times to come. He seldom went to the office and seemed happier in himself and more enterprising than he had before he had gone away.

Philip did not take part in these trips made by my father. A place was found for him at once and, when I complained of his absences, I was told that he was now one of the junior staff and that we must not expect to see him except on Sundays.

One of the first things our father did on his return was to arrange a cattle count and Mother, Beattie and I were invited. My father remarked that he would drive in his single buggy and that we three could pack into the double buggy with the parcels of food and the drinks. My mother was an excellent housekeeper. She was, I found, renowned among my father's friends for the manner in which she organised picnics. Now my father was home again, she threw herself into the arrangement of all sorts of dishes for him and saw to the preparation of delicious meats, pies, fruits and vegetables, many of which Beattie and I had never tasted before.

For two days before the date fixed for the cattle count, the whole household at Arcadia was busy. Native baskets were packed and placed ready on the front steps early on the appointed day. Before the sun was well above the horizon, Beattie and I were dressed in our riding habits and high leather boots and Mother, who was in a linen coat and skirt, met us in the porch. As soon as I was ensconced on the front seat of the buggy, a plate basket was placed between my knees and a tray of little pies on my lap. Jack and Albert ran through the house from the kitchen or the pantry carrying one thing after another. All sorts of baskets of food were perched between and on top of Mother, Beattie and me and in the back seat of the buggy and bottles, fruits and vegetables were placed on my father's trap. When, at last, we moved slowly off, there was not a nook or cranny in either carriage which had been left empty.

On the long drive up into the hills, Mother, who seemed to be younger and more enthusiastic than I had ever known her, told us stories of visits she had paid to the centre of Jamaica when she had first come out as a young bride. On one occasion she and my father had driven far into the mountains and had been entertained royally by a Scottish couple who had settled in a lonely valley far from a railway or main road. After a fifty-mile drive she had washed and changed and come down to find the table in the dining room laden with food. At one end was a half sheep, at the other a turkey; on one side were two little sucking pigs, on the other two guineafowl and an enormous pie and peacock with its tail feathers arranged as a fan. All this was arranged for four people, the old Scotsman and his wife and my young father and mother, for the sons and daughters of the house and their descendants were not considered sufficiently important to dine with the guests and so waited outside for their share of the feast.

'What,' I asked my mother, 'did you eat?'

'A little slice of guineafowl and a piece of white yam cooked on the embers,' replied Mother. 'But the men had a good meal.'

I spent the greater part of the drive to Home Castle (the estate on which the count was to take place) thinking of this feast in which my mother had partaken twenty-five years before. It was not so much the food which interested me as the old couple who had settled in that lonely valley in their early youth and who had made it a land of plenty.

Jamaica, I knew, was not now the prosperous island it had been. I had heard many complaints of hard times from my father and his friends. The price of sugar was beginning to drop and the agents of big German firms who came twice a year to buy the casks of highly scented rum offered every year a lower price. If the sugar estates were finding it difficult to compete with the world's best trade, then all the hill estates which supplied them with cattle, mules and other necessaries must, of course, suffer also.

When we reached Home Castle, there were no signs of hard times. Everything had been prepared on a grand scale. An empty house had been made ready and a little army of black servants stood waiting to unpack the food we had brought and to prepare the breakfast which would be served later.

We found ourselves in an enormous hollow in the land completely surrounded by hills. In the middle of this broad valley were the cattle pens enclosed in pastures. High above them, on a small hill, was the Busha House and stables.

My mother got out at the Busha House and, telling us that she would see us later with the rest of the party, sent Beattie and me off in the buggy to the pens where the counting of the stock was to take place.

As we drew near the pens, we could hear the almost continuous lowing of cattle and shrill neighing of horses and this reached a crescendo as Henry drew up by a huge fig tree under which four or five buggies were already assembled.

I was, by that time, speechless with excitement. The sun was blazing down and the wide space of hard-beaten ground reflected the light dazzlingly. In the distance was a small group of men among whom I could distinguish my father.

Beattie seemed quite calm.

'Come on,' she said. So I walked by her side across the hot space and stood with her while she asked where we should go. The noise from the animals was so great that she had to raise her voice and my father stooped to her ear to answer her. All the men who were assembled looked pleased but none of them were trembling as I was. They may have thought that I was afraid, for one of them took me by the arm and said to my father, 'We must take the young ladies to the stand,' and, in an aside to me, 'There is nothing to be afraid of, the cattle are wild but they all break out in the same way. The cattle boys see to that.'

I listened to what he said and followed eagerly when we all walked, in a body, through the high gates into an enormous walled enclosure. In the middle of the enclosure, which I had guessed to be one of the pens, was a tiny wooden erection with a roof to it and a broad ledge round it on which one could rest one's arms and on which ledgers had been laid.

As soon as we were settled, a black man carrying a big whip came up to the front of the stand and asked 'Big Massa' if the count should begin. My father raised his head from the ledger before him and was just about to reply when there was a shout and we all turned round.

The big gates behind us were once more flung open and a man in yellow trousers, a white coat and a panama hat came shambling in.

'Wait a moment,' said my father, 'it's Herr Bauer.'

We all stood still. After my first glance round I averted my face and stared in front of me. I had forgotten Herr Bauer and that he would, of course, be here to see the cattle counted. During the slight commotion which followed on the stand and while the men were moving to allow room for the newcomer, the black cattleman with the whip approached quite close and stood below me. He was coiling and uncoiling his whip and watching the row of white men above him. As Herr Bauer elbowed his way rudely among us, he muttered, 'Red ant him ting,' and I could see his white teeth gleam as he spoke and the contemptuous look on his face.

I distinctly heard what the cattleman said and I think Herr Bauer did too for he gave a sort of snarl as he flung his arms across the ledge beside me and shouted down to the man to begin the count without further delay.

The black man, however, paid no attention to the attorney. He was a tall, fine-looking man and there was something independent and careless in the way he walked down the line until he came opposite my father. There he paused and once more repeated his question politely, 'Big Massa, him ready?'

My father nodded without looking up and immediately the cattleman sprang quickly away cracking his whip loudly. This must have been a signal, for, at once, the barriers into a narrow corridor were let down and, with shouts and calls, a group of Indian cows and calves came charging through.

These were the first of hundreds of animals which galloped past. Some young cows became separated from their calves and, lowing piteously, attempted to break back to rejoin them. Others, older ones, galloped unconcernedly by followed by a fine-looking yearling and a baby calf; this was, evidently, not the first time they had passed and they showed no fear. Now and then a big bull shouldered his way through, bellowing furiously, his head down and his eyes on the men around him. As each animal raced by, the head cattleman, facing us at the mouth of the corridor, called out a name: 'Cow Rosie', 'Cow Miriam', or 'Cow Ada'.

'Yearling steer Marlborough'. 'Yearling heifer Cressida'. 'Bull calf Mahomet'.

My father and his friends seized their pencils and began to tick off each animal on the ledgers lying open before them. I had no pencil and so had time to look about me and notice the things which were happening so rapidly. Never once did the headman falter or hesitate for a name and soon my mind was reeling in a helpless attempt to repeat after him all those odd familiar titles.

It was very hot. After a time I shut my eyes and, when I opened them again, the first thing I saw was Herr Bauer's hand lying on the ledger beside me.

It was a horrible hand, burnt in patches, and covered over the back and down each finger with thick red hairs; I would have preferred to have been beside anyone else and squeezed against the extreme end of the stand in an effort to leave a space between us. Twice I stood upright and thought seriously of making an escape, either down the stand or under the rail on my left, but I had not the courage to do either of these things. An hour or more must have passed in this way. There were, I could see, rows of pencil marks on Herr Bauer's sheet. The first tense excitement among my neighbours began to lessen and some of them lit cigarettes. At longer and longer intervals the animals charged through and still I had not made up my mind to move. Then, suddenly, a burst of shouting and a movement in the enclosure attracted my attention. Two of the big bulls had begun to fight.

I had been so occupied with my own thoughts that I was the last to notice this for, when I looked up, they were already quite close. Round and round the huge beasts circled, bellowing and charging. They were, I could see, equally matched and neither would give way. Dozens of cattle boys appeared from all sides and did their best to separate them but in vain. And the cries of the men and the roars of the bulls were, all at once, terrifying.

I had not noticed that, on the first alarm, all my companions had escaped by the far end of the stand and had rushed, in a body, to safety. I stood alone, clinging to the ledge, staring stupidly at the grey straining backs which circled within a foot or two of me. Then, very quickly, the head cattleman whom I had noticed at the beginning of the count and who had called out all the names, jumped lightly onto the stand and, picking me up in his arms, ran with me across the open space and helped me climb up onto a high wall. Having reached this point of vantage, I sat there quite still watching the scene below me. One of the bulls had been pushed backwards and had sat down on the end of the stand, demolishing it completely. The other one, surprised by the unaccountable collapse of anything so stable, broke off the encounter to stare and the black boys, taking advantage of this lucky chance, separated the two enormous animals and soon had them trotting amiably in different directions. Perched high above the scene of confusion, I thought what reserve and self-control these bulls now showed. They were, in a minute, detached and indifferent. The boys' cries changed into a sort of musical two-note call, their whips ceased to crack and the last company of cows and calves cantered out onto the common. My father walked round the outside of the pen and, standing below me with outstretched arms, told me to jump down. The cattle count was over.

At lunch the men made light of the mischance and chaffed each other on the celerity with which they had left the stand, crossed the open space and reached safety. The whole occurrence soon became to them an amusing adventure. But, in spite of the good lunch Mother had provided, I did not enjoy my meal. Herr Bauer set to work at once to abuse the head cattleman. He said the bulls should never have come near enough to each other to fight and that the whole thing was a case of crass mismanagement. 'You must dismiss him,' he said to my father bitterly.

The other guests said nothing but the merry conversation ceased. I did not think they liked Herr Bauer; they never chaffed or joked with him and that, with them, seemed to mean a lot. As for me, I thought of the remark the black man had made at the beginning of the count when Herr Bauer had arrived late and I realised what was meant by 'red ant him ting'.

That night, when we got home, I was so tired that I could hardly keep my head up. In the afternoon we had taken a long ride and, with the excitement of the count, the long day in the open air and the many people we had seen and talked with, I felt that I had had enough.

Wearily I walked through the hall and up the stairs to bed but Beattie stopped at the sideboard where the letters were always laid ready; and, before I reached the turn in the stairs, she called me back. 'Come here,' she said softly. 'It's come.'

Half dazed, I ran down again and in another second Beattie had put a letter in my hands. It was addressed to me and stamped with a Jamaica postmark. It was indeed the long-expected letter from Mr Biggar. There seemed something contrary in its long delay and arrival on a day which was already full to overflowing. Up in our bedroom, I opened the letter, read it and passed it across to Beattie. This is what it said:

Dear Miss Lewes – I have been very much interested in your MSS. What you have written is really an attempt to develop a theory of Human Nature: an attempt which, at various periods in history, a great many celebrated people have made and, I am afraid, generally failed in.

Every living human is so infinite and various, both from all others, and from himself at different moments of his life, that it is impossible to pin him down in a formula. For instance, one may know a person for years, and then one day discover some new aspect of him, one possibly which he, least of all, would have suspected. Then two people react on each other and alter and modify each other; and these modifications vary with each individual person. In your essay, I know, you admit the modifications of one type through the influence of some other. But then, what is the ultimate basis from which each type starts. 'Character,' you write 'is the root of all.' But what is character? Is it something one is born with – inherits at the start? Or do the circumstances of our lives make it for us or is it the result of both these influences? What I mean is that your classification of people is too narrow, too arbitrary. What you say of each type is very true but it is 'true only in outline' as you admit yourselves; and it is what is personal and peculiar, the manners of character which are the really important things to grasp in understanding people.

Perhaps I shall make my meaning clear by putting the case thus: take any half dozen people whom you know really well, whose lives you can watch, the peculiarity of whose personalities you are sufficiently familiar with to be in a position to note the daily, hourly changes in them. Try to describe them, not as instances of a general rule, but as themselves, try to describe them so that people who had never met them would recognise them as convincingly real. If you tried to do this, you would, I think, realise how wide your theory was of the actual facts of Human Nature.

I think your essay also fails from your tendency to generalise from your particular acquaintances to a type, instead of endeavouring to see in each individual a universal element. For that (in spite of all appearances to the contrary) exists in all of us, and is, perhaps, ultimately the only real thing.

Yours sincerely,

J. Biggar

P.S. If you have two combined classes, you must have twelve.

Waves and waves of thought swept over me. I was in a deep resounding sea which deafened and stunned me and rolled me helplessly along with it. I suppose what I heard was my own blood drumming in my ears. Beattie's voice came from far away saying, 'Of course, he is right. There must be twelve combined classes. Why did we not think of that before? You see there must be three suave combined characters, three pleasing, three simple and three animal. It should have been obvious.'

It was like Beattie to seize on the one point in the whole letter which gave us practical encouragement.

There were only two chairs in my bedroom; these we placed opposite each other and, seating ourselves on them, knee to knee, we discussed, sentence by sentence, the new perspective which Mr Biggar had suggested to us. Beattie's quiet voice went on and on, and on and on went my thoughts and hopes and wishes, until, with the moonlight on the floor, the bubbling of frogs in the pond and the pulsing of the whole Jamaican night, they merged, in my tired mind, into confusion.

CHAPTER 6

Oxford (1)

M R BIGGAR'S LETTER revived our interest in the theory. It became once more of paramount interest to us and filled our minds to the exclusion of everyday affairs. Our absent-mindedness and the long hours we again began to spend on the verandah must have displeased our parents and informed them that we were not the carefree girls we had been when we first came out from England. What they attributed our condition to I do not know, but that they resented it and considered it bad for us soon became apparent. My mother spared time from her household duties to devise jobs for us and my father asked why we had given up our afternoon rides. The escaped prisoner had long since been safely back in prison, so brushing aside any fear of such a danger occurring again, he ordered Henry to send round our horses that very afternoon without 'William and his mule'.

This order of theirs was not, at first, easy to perform, for the horses, when they came round, were so fat that their girths would not meet the saddles and had to be lengthened by odd pieces of string. As we rode sedately down the drive and out onto the road, I told Beattie that she looked like a bung on a barrel and that I hoped none of our friends would see us. This so exasperated her that she whacked St Hilaria, causing her to buck half-heartedly but with sufficient energy to burst her bonds. For a day or two, to keep up a slow trot, we were forced to take more exercise than our lazy mounts, but in time they were reduced to normal proportions and rides once more became exhilarating.

There were days which went gloriously right from start to finish, when no deed, however small or insignificant, was anything but perfect and no person anything but kind. But, then again, there were days which went wrong from early tea until bedtime, when every deed was contrary and all thoughts confused. On such days the first sparkle of the sun through the casuarina trees on the back drive was a forlorn hope.

On this morning my mother said, 'Miss Murry, the dress-maker, is coming up from Falmouth for a week. Henry will take the small buggy to fetch her and Peterkin will drive your father to the office in the double buggy.' I felt as if just such a hopeless day had dawned.

The truth was that I loathed being fitted. Long before the dress was finished, I disliked it and everything to do with it. It was bad enough to find oneself in the hands of a real dressmaker in England, but it was a thousand times worse if the fitter happened to be a fat woman with her mouth full of pins and her breath blowing her nostrils in and out like a pair of bellows.

Miss Murry was not a real dressmaker, she was a sewing woman. And, instead of fitting human beings, she should, I felt, have been attending to sofas. To be trained to make sofa covers when there are no sofas to make covers for must be one of those occasions on which people are justified in saying, 'She is educated out of her sphere.' Of course, as Miss Murry was only a sofa coverer, heaps of alterations had to be made during the making of the dress. When, on the morning after her arrival, my mother said, 'I think, Miss Murry, you might give a little more fullness here,' all the pins had to come out before she could reply, 'Yes, Madam, the young lady is growing a beautiful bust.'

This remark put the finishing touch to my feelings of annoyance. I hated 'figures' anywhere, either back or front, and the moment I was able to escape I rushed upstairs and, wrapping myself into my cretonne box cover, I rolled on the verandah.

Unfortunately, Princess, the housemaid, happened to come out at that moment and shrieked, 'Lars me, Jesus, de young Misses am rollin' wid a so so kiver on her back.'

Everyone thought I must be mad and I had to scramble to my feet and explain why I had been discovered in such an undignified position. However, Mother only said, 'You can bring your box cover down and let Princess iron it when she has done the bedrooms.'

And, with this, everything calmed down.

Rachel Reay was staying with us at this time. She was the eldest of the Reays and the most concentrated. Had all the other Reays (and there were eleven of them) been boiled in a vat, Rachel would have been just as much a Reay as the rest of the dozen collected out of the vat. I liked the other eleven Reays, but I liked them better unconcentrated.

We four, Mother, Beattie, Rachel and I, sat sewing in the morning room one day. Rachel passed the time telling us of her brothers and sisters and we learnt many things of Bill, my friend, which we had not known before. He had once, she said, gone swimming in the river near their house and had forgotten his shirt and tie and had never noticed their absence until next morning when he came to dress.

Later at lunch my father said to Rachel, 'Your father was a tartar. I can remember driving up to your place and seeing your brothers and sisters running here and there like a lot of rats, looking for a place to hide. What is your mother doing with them now?'

I knew that Rachel's father had been dead some years, but she showed no feeling at this remark. It seemed that she laughed a lot although she did not appear as amused as one might have expected considering the noise she made. I guessed that she had 'pleasing' in her from the ready way she responded with a bright answer to any question. And yet I felt sure she must have some 'animal' too.

'The three youngest are at school in England,' she replied. 'Rupert has taken Bill, as you know, and the others are doing the best they can on our estates.'

Again my mind wandered to our theory and I thought it surprising that she should sound so complacent. There was no trace of sympathy in her voice for those of her brothers who had been denied an education during a tyrannical father's lifetime.

'Rupert went to Cambridge, didn't he?' asked my father.

'Yes, Rupert and I went to England,' replied Rachel and, by the tone of her voice, I felt sure that I had been right and that she did not mind because she had been one of the lucky ones.

My father continued unconcernedly, 'Well, it's a pity he did not send the others too. Now it's too late.'

A cackle of laughter came from Rachel and I remembered a Sunday when Rupert and Bill had come to lunch with us. I always looked forward to seeing Bill and listening to him too, for he invariably had something interesting to say. On that particular Sunday, he had teased Beattie and me and accused us of being silent at meals.

'You two girls are as silent as water buffalo,' he said, 'yet up on the verandah you chatter like parrots. Why don't you give them something to think about in the dining room?'

'Oh I can't,' I had replied earnestly, 'I have nothing of interest to say.'

'Well, look something up in the papers. That is what I do.'

After that I always noticed how he waited for a pause in the conversation and how cleverly he brought out his piece of news. He deserved, I thought, a good education much more than Rachel who seemed to be able to do nothing but cackle.

At three, Beattie and I took Rachel for a ride. When we reached Lookout Village which was on the Upper Road and not far from the front gates, Beattie said to me, 'Which way shall we go today?' and, knowing by this that she was at a loss and hoped that I would make a suggestion, I said quickly, 'To the view.'

Had I waited to think or consider what I was about to say, I do not think I should have mentioned the view, but Rachel made all roads uninteresting and I let out the first thought which came uppermost in my mind. The place we called 'the view' was a small rough hill which jutted out to the right from the Upper Road and from it one could look out over Falmouth to the sea. Why this spot should have reminded us of England and thus have earned its name, I do not know. Our memories were strange things and those places which recalled beautiful thoughts were stranger still. England lay to the north-east of Jamaica and our hill faced the sinking sun but, all the same, this rough scrub-covered spot always brought back memories of our Dorset home. On this afternoon in February, nightingales were beginning to sing after the heat of the day, little birds were rustling in the bushes and, far away to the west, the sun had scattered a path of shining stars on the waves. I fell into a dream and, in my dream, I was with my brothers at home. It was summer in England, I thought. Victor and

Somerville, my two younger brothers, were pulling a boat onto the beach in the cove. Their shoes and stockings were off and their knickerbockers rolled up to their thighs. From where I sat on a rock, I could watch the waves rushing over their bare feet and hear the grate of the boat's keel on the shingle. 'Come and help,' called Victor. 'What are you sitting there for?' Yes, what was I doing sitting, watching when I might be helping, feeling the cool water running over my feet and the weight of the boat against my shoulder? The picture was so clear that I could hear their peremptory voices and see the beads of perspiration on their sunburnt faces. In another moment, I should have been with them, pulling and struggling and then, all in a moment, I was back in Jamaica, six thousand miles away, unwillingly translated. I suppose that I looked lost for Rachel began to speak in her interfering way. 'Thinking of him?' she said.

I looked at her sitting so stiffly on her pony, her hands on her reins and her bright, birdlike eyes fixed on me. What, I wondered, had she understood? I suppose I laughed in a self-conscious way. There seemed nothing to do or say but, when we guided our horses down the rough path and onto the Upper Road, the Jamaican view was swimming.

Time passed; a fortnight later Rachel went home and soon a big change took place. Philip was promoted and given charge of a small sugar estate called Oxford. When he wrote to say he had a small spare bedroom furnished and that we might pay him a visit, both Beattie and I felt elated. Permission for us to go was soon granted and, with our nightclothes and toothbrushes tied up in bundles and strapped to our saddles, we rode away on our first visit to Oxford. Philip met us in the estate's yard and walked up with us to the Busha House. I thought he looked well in his white drill coat and breeches, brown riding boots and pith helmet.

A sugar estate was a little world to itself. In the north of the island where we lived, sugar cane only grew profitably in certain areas or in pockets of land between and among the hills. Oxford estate, my brother's new charge, lay at the end of a long ridge where the land fell away to the low levels, mangrove swamps and the Martha Brae river. The estate consisted of 500 acres, but of these, only about 130 were cane pieces and they were broken up and divided from each other by steep ridges, rocks and rough pastures. To work such a property, a large herd of working cattle was required.

The first thing I remember about Oxford was its cattle pen full of animals of all sorts and sizes. The Busha House stood on a rocky hill and, from it, one had a splendid view of the sugar works, the yard and pens.

'How many cattle do you have?' I said, turning in my saddle to look down at the pens, as we climbed the hill to the house.

'One hundred and eighty-nine,' Philip answered. 'And the field bookkeeper has to know them all.'

'Could Beattie or I be made bookkeepers?' I asked with excitement.

'You two can take it in turns, week by week, when you come to stay,' he said. And then, as if he thought I might imagine my new job was to be nothing but a game, he added, 'But you will have to know all those cattle by name and be able to catch out the drivers who use any one animal two days running before you are any use.'

I slipped off Victoria's back and gave my reins to a black boy who came running up to take the two horses. Then we unstrapped our bundles and climbed up a long flight of stone steps to the house. Like many of the old-fashioned Jamaican houses, it was built a storey above ground. Underneath were store rooms and servants' sleeping quarters. Above these, approached only by two flights of steps, was the main part of the building and, crowning all, was a wide, sloping hurricane roof.

I deposited my bundle in the bedrooms which had been prepared for us and then took a look round my brother's new home. The centre was occupied by a large, airy dining room, out of which the bedrooms, two on each side, opened. To the north, there was a long strip of a room which embraced the width of the house and which was furnished with a few rocking chairs and an unpadded sofa. This was the drawing room and, leaning my elbows on the windowsill, I looked down on the pens where the cattle were eating their evening meal of cane tops. Some were white, I noticed, some fawn in colour like the pure-bred Mysores I had seen at the cattle count at Home Castle, some were black and white or brown or black. Some had branching horns but only a few seemed outstanding in any way in their shape or colour.

When Philip came and joined me at the neighbouring window, I asked him, 'Why is it necessary to know all their names?'

'Because,' he answered, 'the drivers always take out the quiet ones and leave the unbroken ones in the pens if they are not watched. And no steer, fed as these are, can stand being worked every day.'

I stared at the animals below me until Beattie came in and said she thought dinner must be ready and that I had better wash my hands and brush my hair.

At dinner I asked her if she thought she could learn the names of the steers. But all she said was, 'I suppose there are other things a field bookkeeper can do.'

Philip laughed at my discomfiture and said, 'Beattie can always count the canes and supervise the pic'ny gang and we can leave the herd to you.'

It seemed hard to leave the busy sugar works the next morning but we had only received permission to stay one night. So we packed our bundles and, presently, our horses picked their way carefully down the steep road to the yard. There, early as it was, all was bustle and life. The space in front of the works was already half full of sugar canes tied in bundles and placed in heaps ready for the mill. I drew up to watch the feeders untie these bundles and throw the canes onto the moving platform. To me there was something fascinating in the perfect interplay between the different parts of the machinery. The slowly moving ribbon of canes carried my eyes, again and again, up the platform and over the shining surface of the big rollers where the juice was squeezed out and the remaining pith and husk dropped to a pit beneath. Far below, I could see other black men raking this trash away and, out in the sunny yard, the pic'ny gang was spreading what was later to feed the furnaces.

As we rode away, we had to pull to one side to give place to laden wagons which were bringing in still more canes from the fields. All these people, the feeders, the men who tended the rollers, the rakers of trash, the piccaninnies and the running drivers of the bullock wagons seemed to be part of a smoothly working system of which I wanted to be part.

When we got back to Arcadia, my mother said we were sunburnt and that we had better bathe our faces in milk and put on blue veils when we rode or drove in future. I suppose I was tiresome and obstinate for I remember I said I would rather not ride at all if I were forced to wear a blue veil. And it was not until Beattie gave me some good advice that I hunted out my veil and fastened it onto my riding hat.

'You had better do as you are told,' she said when we were up in our bedrooms.

'Why?' I asked, as I stripped off my jacket and vest and reached out for a bath towel. 'Well, of course I ought to do what I am told but why, particularly, now?'

The last part of my remark was muffled in the nice dry towel with which I began to rub myself vigorously.

'Because,' Beattie's voice coming distantly as she raised her head from the wash basin, 'there is going to be a dance.'

'A dance?' I dropped my towel and walked into her room. 'But will I go? You know I am not out yet.'

'Well, not altogether ... but partly. Mother is taking me up to a ball at King's House next month and I am having a new dress from England for it. But the Reays are giving a dance at Retreat and they have specially asked if you may go.'

Immediately I was filled with remorse for the unkind things I had thought and said about Rachel.

'Did Rachel ask me?' I asked.

Beattie took out clean underclothes and proceeded to put them on before she answered. 'She brought the message,' she said, at last, 'but it's Rupert and Bill who are giving the dance and Alice is acting as hostess for them.'

'Oh,' I exclaimed. The necessity to thank someone for his or her kindness was therefore transferred from Moneague Pen, where Rachel and the bulk of the Reay family lived, to Retreat where Rupert and Bill kept house together. 'Do you think it was Bill?' I added.

'I dare say, but you needn't get so excited. You can thank him next Sunday when he comes to lunch. There are a lot more things I have to tell you.'

Beattie was now dressed and, while I hurried into my clothes, she went on to tell me that a young man called Mr Cameron was coming to stay with us. His estates lay next to my father's and he was visiting Jamaica to inspect them. All my questions as to when and why he was coming to us were answered quickly and details of other kinds given to me. I heard further that, while Beattie and my mother were to be in Kingston, Alice Reay would stay with me at Arcadia and that we would have a trap and pony to drive since Alice was not able to ride.

'When did you hear all this?' I asked

'Yesterday, when you were out walking with Bundle, but, for goodness sake, don't say you know. Mother will tell you everything herself in her own time.'

All this information and the fact that Beattie had kept it from me tended to depress me. I know that I was four years younger than her but to find out that a series of important events had been decided without my having heard of them was disconcerting. The news made me feel that I was, in a way, on probation. It was therefore with a sense of insecurity that I entered on this whirl of gaiety. With a view to preparing myself for the part I would have to play, I went to the library and pulled out Darwin's *The Origin of Species* and, for the time being, forgot all about Oxford and the proposed dance. After reading this for a while my mind wandered back to the theory and to the people who came and went at our house. I decided that Rachel must be pleasing-animal. Philip, Lucy and Herr Bauer were, I knew, pleasing, Catherine was pleasing-suave, I wondered what Mr Cameron would turn out to be.

CHAPTER 7

Mr Cameron

I WAS SHY OF MR CAMERON when he arrived. He was a stockily built man of twenty-two with a slow, rather ponderous way of speaking. I thought he was not over-quick mentally, that he liked to be quite sure what he thought before he expressed an opinion and also that he rather suspected other people of trying to rush him into decisions. Still, from the very first moment I saw him, I felt that he was reliable and that I liked him. He was fair, English in appearance and what people call 'transparently honest'. Perhaps it was this honesty which made him slow in speech and perhaps truth was more important to him than any good impression he might make on others.

A few days after his arrival, at my mother's instigation, Beattie and I took him to Mahogany Hall. The ride there was, as far as we humans were concerned, an almost silent one. I left what conversation there was to my sister. She received little help from Mr Cameron and soon gave up her half-hearted attempts to amuse him and, when finally we reached the common at Mahogany Hall, tired of the long silence, she tore off down the common in a helter-skelter style, her horse's white mane and tail streaming in the wind.

Lucy and Catherine seemed delighted to see us. They gave us a warm welcome and ordered their horses to be brought round after tea so that they might accompany us part of the way back. Charles, their brother, who had, on a previous occasion, made the ridiculous remark about Bundle, came to the barbecue to see us off. I was the last to mount and, as he handed me the reins, he said, 'Mind the cattle. I did not know you were coming over this afternoon and they are on the common. Did you see them as you came up?'

'No.'

'Well, perhaps they are at the other end.'

Charles seemed anxious to be off about his own business and Lucy was waiting for me so I walked my horse soberly down the drive thinking of what he had said to me. After my experience at the Home Castle cattle count, I would not have attempted to go near the cattle on foot but, mounted, there seemed little to fear from them. I realised for the first time that, on our previous visits, the common had always been empty of all animals. When the drive gates shut behind us, we soon saw that the large herd of cattle was scattered over just that portion of the common which we had to cross. With the intention of causing as little disturbance among them as possible, Lucy suggested that our horses should walk and, in compliance with her wishes, they did so. Catherine, Beattie and Mr Cameron were in front and Lucy and I about twenty yards behind. From the first it was obvious that the stock were interested in us. Even the big bull raised his head and stared. They were all pure Indian cattle and as beautiful in form and colour as those which I had seen at the cattle count. Lucy began to tell me a story of a calf which, when operated upon, had revealed a lump in its stomach as big and hard as a cricket ball.

'It was all hair,' said Lucy. 'You see they lick and lick ... '

At this moment, Victoria swerved and a cow, with lowered head, galloped past, missing her by a yard. At the same time I became aware of some sort of concerted action among the cattle which seemed to centre on the three riders in front. Just before the cow charged and Victoria had swerved, I had been looking at the old bull. He was nearly twice as large as the other animals and had a large hump on his shoulders but, for all his size and weight, he looked as if he would be quick on his feet. While Catherine, Beattie and Mr Cameron advanced, he had remained motionless but the moment they passed him and their eyes were no longer on his he made a low sound like a moan and at once the herd had started in motion, immediately some had run in front of Lucy and me, some on either hand and some, like the cow who had charged Victoria, had galloped between the two parties cutting us off from each other. Lucy cried out to warn me and at the same time her pony reared.

My thoughts started jumping here and there. For a second I looked at Lucy. I could see all the freckles standing out plainly over the bridge of her nose and under her eyes. Beads of perspiration sprang out above her mouth which was open and formed a dark patch in her face. She had reined in and come to a standstill. Kicking Victoria as hard as I could, I set her into a gallop for, in the situation, it seemed dangerous to remain still and, loosening the thong of my whip, I made a cut at the cow which had frightened Lucy's pony. The cow must have felt this for she bellowed loudly.

With the exception of Lucy's cry and the bull's strange message to the herd, this was the first sound and it seemed, for me, to break the spell. 'Gallop,' I yelled. And I began to crack my whip furiously. I suppose I hit Victoria more frequently than I hit anything else for she plunged to and fro but, at the same time, I let her have her head and complete freedom to move, which was as well for it enabled her to avoid the cattle which were now racing in all directions. The loud cracks of my whip startled the other horses and set them in motion. Beattie's horse went off at a great pace and, finding a gap in the herd, led the way through and off down the common.

Lucy now had her supplejack out and, with it, she belaboured her pony, urging it by cries and blows to escape; but, again and again, the young cattle overtook her and it seemed that one of them would throw her pony down. To prevent this I galloped once around her, shouting and brandishing my whip. Then, as suddenly as they had begun, the cattle gave up the chase. I was in no state to take any notice of their further actions. I was streaming with perspiration and my vest was sticking to my back. Victoria was black with sweat and flecked with foam along her neck. As we galloped to the lower gate, it came into my mind that the cows had been the most aggressive but that, had they got any of us down, the old bull would not have been far behind.

When we all drew up at the gate, Mr Cameron pulled in beside me. He was very crimson.

'I didn't know they were dangerous,' he said apologetically.

'Neither did I,' I replied.

From that moment I lost my feeling of shyness with him. There is something friendly about a shared danger and, when Lucy and Catherine had left us at the top of First Hill with all sorts of expressions of regret for the episode on the common, I turned to our guest quite naturally and asked him if he did not think Jamaica a wonderful place, for I could now feel the fascination of this lovely island. That evening, as we rode home from Mahogany Hall, I felt extraordinarily happy. The evening chorus of sound had begun. Bullfrogs were throbbing in the hollows, birds were singing and insects were chirping loudly. I could remember when this overpowering hubbub of sound, which took place before and after the sun set, had frightened me. That evening the same thing exhilarated me and raised my spirits to a pitch of excitement comparable to a nervous anticipation of something fine and Beattie, Mr Cameron and I chattered like children.

'You did the right thing,' said Beattie to St Hilaria.

'She did indeed,' said I, pleased with all the world.

'I do believe that Catherine was afraid, and they are her own cattle.'

'And Lucy, what about the freckles on her nose? I could have counted them if the cows had given me time.'

Slowly, as the night fell, little chains of light came out; in the bamboo clumps these lights wove patterns and, where the trees made dark patches, they shone like stars.

'Are those fireflies?' asked Mr Cameron.

'No, peenies!' said Beattie. 'We shall have rain. I have never seen so many.'

As we walked our horses to cool and calm them, for they were still nervous and excited, our conversation gradually ceased until all I could hear was the fall of hooves on the road, the creak of leather and the ring of iron on stone when one of the horses, growing tired, stumbled.

Victoria's neck was wet to my fingers and soon I had to trot to warm her. Then the land breeze came up behind us and, as it crept under my coat, it made my vest feel cold and uncomfortable against my skin. And, before we reached home, my companions were like shadows.

CHAPTER 8

Colonel Egerton

O N SATURDAY, a few days later, Colonel Egerton
came to lunch with my parents. I say he came on
Saturday because that was the day on which his
letter arrived, although it was just ten minutes to one on
the following day that his buggy and horses came trotting
round the house and pulled up by the front steps. Some
people seem to arrive from the moment one first hears of
them, while others never put in an appearance until the
lunch bell is ringing and then still remain distant.

That morning at breakfast my father had said: 'Colonel
Egerton is coming to lunch tomorrow. He is a famous
man. He wrapped the colours round his waist, swam
three rivers and brought back news that General Fawcett's
expedition had been surprised and cut to pieces by the
Zulus. He was not more than a lad at the time. He has
never settled since.'

The moment my father said that, Colonel Egerton began
to arrive and he continued to grow until ten minutes to one
on the Sunday. I was dressed and ready in good time
because I did not wish to miss anything.

He jumped out of the buggy the moment it stopped, ran
up the step and greeted my father in a very nice way. He
was as tall as my father but much thinner.

'I am very glad to see you,' said my father. 'Sorry you
can't spend the night,' and they began to talk. I was not
exactly interested in their conversation but let it go flowing

80

along without attempting to picture what they were saying for I wished to think about Colonel Egerton and to make up my mind as to whether he was as real as I had imagined him to be or not. Presently other people arrived; they all got up and went through into the dining room where Jack was opening bottles and pouring out drinks at the sideboard. From where I sat in the porch, I could hear their voices rising, occasionally in bursts of laughter.

When the lunch bell rang they returned to where I was sitting, my mother and Beattie came downstairs and we all walked into the dining room and took our places at the table. My one thought was to get beside someone who would not talk too much. I never dreamt that I should sit beside Colonel Egerton but, as it happened, that was exactly what occurred. In avoiding Mr Hemans, another of our guests who generally settled himself down next to me, I found myself two places from my mother and next to the empty chair she was keeping for him.

Mr Hemans would have been a pleasant companion had it not been for a story he had once told of himself. His story was that he had once dined with a connoisseur of food and that he and his friend had agreed, when they sat down to their meal, that they would eat and drink until they were under the table. Of course he made this story sound most amusing and we all laughed a great deal; still, I did not really like it, and neither, I think, did my mother for she said later, 'Your father encourages Mr Hemans.'

Personally, I did not think he needed any encouragement either to tell funny stories or to enjoy his food. Ever since that day I had been unable to forget his stomach and, when we all sat down to a meal and he took his seat beside mine, I was forced to glance round to see how much he was eating. I knew that it was vulgar to think of his stomach but, in spite of that knowledge, I could not help being engrossed by it. He was very stout and, as he breathed, his waistcoat buttons kept rising and falling and I could only watch in fascination. On the occasion of Colonel Egerton's visit, I did not wish to be disturbed by such thoughts and so I avoided Mr Hemans.

We had melon for lunch that day, turtle, turtle eggs, yam, sweet potatoes, cho-chos, peahen, fried plantain, avocado pears and finally coconut pudding. I remember it all quite clearly. It was a man's luncheon party, as so many of ours were. The conversation at the other end of the table turned on Mysore cattle versus black cattle. My father believed in Mysore cattle which came from India and were not affected by the ticks; but one of the guests had lately imported a black bull from England and he gave many reasons to prove that the black bull and his progeny were more suitable to the climate than the Mysore. I had heard all these arguments so many times and at such length that, even on those days when there was nothing else to listen to, I found it difficult to work up any interest in them.

My mother's conversations, on the other hand, never ran in fixed lines and neither, it seemed, did Colonel Egerton's; so I had plenty to do in following them in and out among places and people of whom I had never heard. No one spoke to me and I was content to sit silent. I suppose that, had I thought definitely about it and had anyone asked me, I should have said that I expected the end of lunch to be the same as the beginning. I knew that the cattle would, probably, give place to rum and sugar or even to citrus fruits and seedless oranges. Mr Seymour, who sat on my mother's other hand, would look across at me about the time the coconut pudding came in and say, 'Which is the one who is such a pal of my niece?' and I would reply 'Me,' for his niece in England was a great friend of mine and had been since I was nine years old.

The conversation at the other end of the table did turn to sugar as I had expected, my mother did turn her attention to Mr Seymour, but nothing else fell out as I had imagined it would. Instead, the most extraordinary thing that had ever happened to me occurred.

I had begun to play a game. Colonel Egerton was sitting silent and his hand was lying next to me by his forks so I pretended to slip my fingers out and along the table to his. I wanted to touch him, quite lightly, and then escape back to my place. Just as I was about to touch him, he moved his hand to take mine in his. I was startled and looked up to find he was smiling at me.

'I'm sorry,' I whispered.

'Why?' he asked.

'I don't know.'

'Neither do I.' When he said that, I felt sure he was laughing at me but I am not certain that I was right. One part of my mind went on listening to my mother speaking to Mr Seymour, the other half waited in suspense. In the middle of a funny story related to Mr Hemans, Colonel Egerton asked me another question.

'How old are you?'

'Seventeen ... no, sixteen.' The words were jumped out of me as if they had been pushed by a spring.

'Sixteen. Sad. I am afraid that is not old enough.' And quickly he released my imaginary fingers and put his hand into his pocket.

'Well,' he continued, 'here is something to remember me by. This stamp has a history attached to it.' And from a note case he drew a long-shaped postage stamp which had been franked. All my brothers had, at one time or another, collected stamps and one had amassed as many as six thousand but I had never seen one like this.

'A man went to prison for that stamp,' he added, 'and he is still doing time.'

After saying this he turned away from me and addressed my father down the table.

'I have just given your daughter a postage stamp which has an interesting story connected with it,' and he proceeded to tell of a postmaster in a small state in Africa who had issued postage stamps to augment his income.

Immediately the conversation about rum and sugar ceased and everyone joined in making humorous remarks about the postmaster who had gone to prison. But, as they were the sort of remarks men make when they want to be funny, there is no need for me to repeat them, even were I able to do so.

I held the stamp. Not old enough for what, I wondered, and how old was Colonel Egerton? His chin and nose were beautiful and he had no grey in his hair above his ears. Then how old was he?

'Forty-nine,' he whispered, with only the shortest of short pauses in his description of Africa and the natives.

His whisper answered my question but it did nothing to elucidate the puzzle. I was as confused as to his meaning and as uncertain of my feelings for him as I had been before he spoke. I knew I liked him and I knew that he had, in some way, penetrated my defences but I could not have said whether I liked this or hated it, whether I was frightened or very, very happy.

During the rest of the lunch I held my breath, or only drew it in or let it out as slowly as possible, in the hope that in doing so I should be able to keep my thoughts to myself.

When everyone rose from the table I ran upstairs to the verandah, put my head down on the cool iron railing and tried to think of the hummingbirds which were building a nest in the stephanotis. I never saw Colonel Egerton again, but I often remembered him and his flag and imagined myself rolled up in its blue and white and red folds where only quick thoughts like his could reach me.

Oddly enough, however, the most definite impression which that luncheon party left on my mind was that Colonel Egerton reminded me of my mother; he had the same quick way of jumping to conclusions as she had and was, I felt sure, just as particular. My mother thought much of other people's opinions on social matters and laid much stress on cleanliness but she had another side to her character. Both she and Colonel Egerton were imaginative and dreamy and, most important of all, intuitive and I felt sure that they must both be simple-pleasing.

CHAPTER 9

Retreat

WHEN MOTHER AND BEATTIE went up to Kingston, Alice came to stay at Arcadia. Strangely enough I never told Alice about our theory, never said one word to her that could give her even an inkling that we had a theory or were more than ordinarily interested in character. Why was I, in her case, reticent? Was it because I feared to evoke that blank look of non-comprehension which appeared on so many faces as soon as one started a conversation which the listener either cannot or will not follow? I had by this time become used to this facial expression, for Beattie and I had tried to explain our theory to several friends and I knew all its miserable stages. First would come polite surprise, then doubt, then an interval of patient courtesy during which one was given an opportunity to acknowledge that one had been talking nonsense and that one faithfully promises not to do so again. Then, if one persisted, came condescension, irritation and exasperation; at which point the listener probably said, 'You really do say the most extraordinary things,' which I consider the most crushing remark I know. That awful phrase made me feel that I really and truly must be peculiar.

No, I never expected anything quite so bad from Alice. She was far too sympathetic to be unkind, far too understanding to remain blank and far too humorous to miss the joke which lurks in every character sketch. My reason for not telling her was quite different. On our last failure, I had made a solemn vow not to speak of our theory to anyone who happened to be staying in the house, not, in fact, to put a strain on a visitor's courtesy. So, although I looked longingly into Alice's large, blue eyes, watched the humorous curve of her wide lips, longed to see quick interest and understanding for me and my theory spring to life in her face, I resisted temptation. It would, I knew, be delightful to have such a listener as she promised to be; it would be even better to make a disciple for the theory; but was it worth the risk? Was it right to put a strain on a helpless friend's politeness? Would it, in fact, be wise to put into words a thought, which might, during the rest of her stay, lie like a living, but unwanted, presence between us?

My decision did not, however, prevent me from dallying with the thought or approaching as near as possible in conversation to my theory's expressions. For instance, when Alice said enthusiastically, 'How jolly your father is!' I replied, 'Yes, isn't he suave?' and waited anxiously for any shade of surprise or doubt on her smiling face. It did not appear. 'Suave, yes,' she continued happily, 'that is just the word. He is a perfect dear.'

My next venture was not quite so successful. Having steered Alice on to the topic of her brothers, a subject which she was never anything but delighted to embark on, I asked her point blank who was her favourite.

'Rupert,' she replied without hesitation. 'He is my special brother.' And then, in deference to my well-known preference for Bill, she went on contentedly, 'But they are all dears and I never stop thinking how lucky I am to have so many. I say there is one for every occasion. A brother for books, a brother for talks and a brother for outdoors.'

'That's Bill,' I broke in enthusiastically. And, forgetting

for the moment my determination to be cautious, I added, 'He's simple.'

'Simple?' she answered doubtfully. 'Do you think so? Most people think him shrewd. All the others say he's wonderful at a bargain, and the Jamaicans just adore him. But, I suppose, there is a side to him which is very young.'

I did not want to descend into that hopeless form of explanation which begins, 'I didn't quite mean that,' for Bill was intuitive and naturally quick like all people we called 'simple' and not in the least childish. So I only said, 'He's natural, isn't he?' meaning natural in opposition to social.

But Alice, being 'pleasing' or partly 'pleasing' herself, misunderstood me.

'Oh! I do hope not,' she said earnestly. 'Of course he hasn't much social experience, only what Rupert has taught him and what he has learnt here at your lunch parties, but he is popular, isn't he?'

Popular – Bill? Of course he was popular; much more so than all the people who were endowed with the qualities we called 'social' and which Alice valued so highly. For, where they were polished, he was genuine, and, where they were polite, he was warm-hearted.

This conversation with Alice made me realise what a lot of explanation our theory would need and what a lot of different meanings other people put to those words we had chosen as titles for our classes.

The third group, pleasing, I introduced with a certain amount of nervousness into our talk. Several of our mutual acquaintances belonged to this class and it was easy to say of one of them, 'She is pleasing.'

But Alice, evidently thinking I had made a slight mistake in my choice of description, replied cheerfully, 'Yes, very pleasant,' and proceeded to attribute to her every nice quality, correct or incorrect, suitable or unsuitable, that she could think of. This mode of discussing our friends, though harmless, made me feel giddy. How could any ordinary girl be so charming, so gifted, so pleasant and so devoid of all disagreeable thoughts and feelings? How, in fact, could any person contain all the best parts of all the four theory classes and none of their corresponding failings? To my mind all this went to show that our theory would be helpful in keeping people within bounds.

I never embarked on the fourth class for whatever would Alice have said had I ventured to call a mutual acquaintance an 'animal'?

A week passed happily in this way with Alice at Arcadia. She and I drove in the new trap and meals at home were cheerful. Mr Cameron became noticeably more talkative. He no longer avoided us girls, as he had done at first, and there were times when he chose to stay with us when he might, without rudeness, have done something else. On the Friday before Mother and Beattie were to come home, Alice got a letter from Bill asking if we could drive up to polo the next day. Alice was as excited as a child and I was pleased at the thought of seeing Bill and watching the ponies, but my enthusiasm was half-hearted for I knew that my father was going to a poker party the next evening and so would not be able to spare us Henry for the long drive.

Inconsiderate as I was in some ways, I never asked my father for permission to do anything he might disapprove of or find it difficult to refuse before outsiders.

'I don't suppose we will be able to go,' I said gloomily.

'Oh, has your father said so?'

'No.'

'Are the horses lame?'

'No.'

'Then why?' Alice's big, blue eyes were full of surprise. To her there were but two obstacles to any project. A man's disapproval and a horse's failure. In her opinion any other difficulty could be overcome by courage and pertinacity. She knew nothing of permission unwillingly given and afterwards retracted.

To my surprise, my father walked into the morning room where we were sewing and said to Alice: 'I have had a line from your brother Rupert saying they are having a game tomorrow to pick the team to play in the cup. I cannot let you have Henry as I am going to a poker party and am taking Mr Cameron with me, but if you like to take Medora in the trap and start in good time, you two can go.' And then, turning to me he added, 'But you must be back in good time.'

Up to a point that expedition, on the following day, was a roaring success. We started early, Medora went well, it was hot but not too hot and we got to Retreat before the game began. Bill took Medora out of the trap at once and, shouting to a boy to take her away and feed her, he propped up the shafts so that we might sit comfortably where we were. In a few minutes, we were surrounded by a jolly crowd of young men.

The game was fast and the four were chosen to represent the club whom I had hoped to see chosen. People so often say, 'So far, so good,' which, to my mind, is a most explicit remark. So far, and even a little further, everything went well with Alice and me. We even had tea up at Retreat and, just before that, were taken to see a new litter of puppies in the stables; but, shortly afterwards, things began to go wrong. In looking back I could see the puppies were a kind of peak of perfection on which we lingered for a few minutes before starting out on a rapid decline from misfortune to misfortune. Had we driven away immediately after tea we might have reached home without adventure and more important still in good time. But, when I looked across at Alice who had just poured out a third cup of tea for Bill and said that I thought we had better be going, Bill had what I suppose he imagined to be a brilliant idea. The moon, he said, would be up early and we should find it much less tiring to drive home in the cool of the evening than to go while the sun was still up; Medora would certainly travel faster and with less exertion to herself and we should have a full moon behind us instead of a sinking sun in our eyes. It all seemed to be a comparison between the heavenly bodies.

He might well have added that, if we took his advice, we should have a longer stay at Retreat but, I suppose, he knew that any mention of his personal wishes would weaken his case so he merely repeated his information about the moon two or three times. At first, remembering my father's injunction, I insisted that we must go at once, but gradually I began to be influenced by Bill's reiterated argument. Rupert and Alice did not ask me to stay, they only continued to point out the disadvantages in my course of action and the obvious advantages in following Bill's suggestion.

As soon as I gave in, cards were brought out and we sat down to play games on the verandah. Rupert said we should have time for one round of 'donkey' and one of 'old maid'. The sun sank as we played two rounds of 'donkey' and five rounds of 'old maid'. Candles were brought out but still the moon showed no sign of rising. There was no luminous background to the hills; it was very dark in the garden.

'I suppose there is no chance of an eclipse tonight?' I said sarcastically to Bill. I had for the moment forgotten all about the time and the importance, to us, of the early rising of the moon. In fact, I had almost become persuaded that the time was dependent on the moon and that, as it had not yet risen, there was no reason for hurry and no cause for anxiety. Then, suddenly, I heard the clock in the dining room strike and I jumped up in fright.

Bill ordered Medora round at once and his own buggy as well so that he might give us a lead to the main road. It was pitch dark and our lamps gave little light. After Bill had sent us on our way with a cheery shout, Medora cut a corner and we went over a big stone. The jerk put out both our lights and left us in complete darkness. From that moment everything went wrong. We had no matches and, when we did succeed in borrowing a box, we found that both the candles had dropped out of the lamp brackets. Later, Medora grew tired, gave up heart and refused to go any faster than a walk. In time, I became desperate and, thinking of my father who would soon be returning from his poker party, I got out of the trap and, taking hold of the bridle, I pulled Medora along while Alice whacked her with the parasol we had taken with us to keep the sun off. In this manner we progressed for nearly five miles. Sometimes I ran and sometimes I walked and all the time Alice urged me and the pony with the parasol and clicks and clucking noises. When the moon eventually rose, I could only feel indignant with her.

The household staff were out waiting for us when we reached home. One of the stable boys took Medora from me. The women, with little cries and ejaculations of fear, fled like a flock of startled birds to their sleeping quarters. Jack and Albert urged us round to the front of the house and up the steps on to the porch. The reason for their alarm was soon apparent. One glance down the drive showed me that the buggy with Henry and my father was, at that moment, returning from the party. I could see the carriage lamps and hear the thud of the horse's hooves on the grass drive. Alice and I ran along the passage and into the back hall. 'Don't, for goodness sake, look at the clock,' I whispered. And, averting my head, I flew upstairs to my room. There I took off my dusty shoes and hat and jumping into bed pulled the sheet up to my chin. With my breath coming in gasps and my heart thumping, I listened to my father's and Mr Cameron's footsteps downstairs. In the back hall they stopped and I heard my father say to Jack, 'Are the young ladies in?'

'Yes, Massa?'

'When did they get in?'

'Don't know, Massa. Sometime, Massa.'

My father did not, as I feared he might, come to my room to assure himself that I was in bed so, after a time, I got up and undressed noiselessly. But the next morning the first question he asked me was: 'What time did you get in last night?'

'I don't know,' I replied with a faint parody of truth. 'But,' I added, in an attempt to bring facts to my assistance, 'I was in bed when you came in.'

I did not tell my father all that had happened. I was fully aware that his annoyance at our failure to return home before he left for his poker party was due, to a great extent, to anxiety on our behalf but I knew also that, had I made a complete statement of our misfortunes, none of these accidents would have excused me in his eyes; and that my real fault lay in having put my trust in other people's opinions and in having deferred to their wishes against my own judgment. My father was like that. He had no sympathy with weakness in others. The whole episode taught me to make up my mind quickly and to do what I thought was right, perhaps not without fear, but certainly without faltering.

CHAPTER 10

The Hague

I ONLY INDISTINCTLY REMEMBER how it came about that my brother happened to be staying at Arcadia when an important event took place which I shall now relate.

Mr Cameron, who Beattie and I had decided was animal like May's father, left us and went to stay with Mr Hemans at The Hague, a property situated a few miles from our house. Alice Reay started off, in a hired buggy, on her seventy-mile drive across Jamaica to Moneague Pen and Mother and Beattie returned from Kingston. I have a vague idea that Herr Bauer, in the weeks preceding and including Mr Cameron's visit, had made Philip's usual Sunday visits to Arcadia at first difficult and then impossible. All Beattie and I knew for certain was that late each Saturday night a note was brought over by a boy on a mule to say that my brother would not be able to come on the following day. Philip made no complaint, but when this had been repeated three Saturdays in succession, my father put his foot down. What Herr Bauer had actually done had been to devise a means to prevent Philip from leaving his estate and my father, when he had satisfied himself that this was the case, insisted that Philip should take three days' holiday at Arcadia without asking permission from the attorney. He became suddenly very suave and refused to allow Herr Bauer to proceed in his harassment of Philip, saying to my mother in our hearing, 'Philip will one day have charge of all my estates and there is no reason why he should be subjected to any unjust treatment now!' And my mother, holding fast to the Victorian ideal that no woman should interfere in her husband's business, made no reply. To me, watching this fight between my father and Herr Bauer and my mother's abstention from interference, it seemed strange that, in a woman's reign, it should have become the vogue for men to be 'manly' and women 'womanly' in this way. I made up my mind from that time that, when I grew up, I should speak when asked for an opinion and act when given an opportunity.

When Philip came over from Oxford for his three days' holiday, I determined to take this chance to tell him what I felt and suspected concerning Herr Bauer. I wanted to waste no more time but to plan with him some means of frustrating Herr Bauer's designs which I had begun to suspect were evil.

Full of my intention I got ready to go with Philip for an early morning ride. Beattie was tired after her stay in Kingston so I knew we should be alone. My horse was suffering from a girth gall but I had been provided with one of the big carriage horses named Warlock. Mother, however, came onto the front steps as we were mounting and handed Philip a note asking him to take it to Mr Cameron. Little unexpected things have a way of complicating matters of greater importance. This request set my mind on a different train of thought and prevented me from carrying out my resolve to speak to Philip about Herr Bauer.

I watched Philip put the note into his breast pocket and, as soon as we were far enough away from the house to make certain that we could not return for instructions, I asked if I must wait at the bottom of the hill while he delivered the note or if I might go with him up to The

Hague. I knew very well that, although Mr Hemans came
to Arcadia frequently, his was not a house to which I would
normally be allowed to go for, as Beattie had explained
to me, Mr Hemans had a mistress and where mistresses
lived no innocent girl could venture. All the knowledge I
possessed on this subject, gleaned from history books, had
taught me that the Roman emperors and the kings of
France had had mistresses. These mistresses had been
young and lovely. In fact their attractive qualities alone
had prepared them for the unregulated position in which
each one of them had eventually found herself. I suppose I
had unconsciously learnt to connect beauty with adultery
and had wondered how Mr Hemans, who was fat and
commonplace in appearance, came to harbour a young and
lovely girl in his Jamaican home and why he didn't marry
her. When I had explained something of all this to Beattie,
she had told me simply that Mr Hemans' mistress was
black.

Here again, I was confronted by a difficulty I had come
up against when trying to understand Herr Bauer's
relations. It seemed strange that we were forced to go to
tea with Herr Bauer and forbidden to accept any invitation
to The Hague.

I raised this with Beattie and she had thought for a time
before answering this conundrum. 'Oh, that's different,'
she had said at last.

But how it came to be different and why the same thing
could in one case be permissible and in the other forbidden
I could not understand. And why Mr Hemans outraged
society and Herr Bauer did not was not clear to me.

Mr Hemans' mistress came regularly to church. She
was a large, glossy black woman with a bold eye and an
assured manner. All I gathered from a scrutiny of her

through my spread fingers as I knelt two pews behind her was the certainty that she could not possibly sully me should I go to tea at The Hague and that, even though Mr Hemans might be blamed for letting such a woman reach a commanding position in his household, he had shown some strength of mind in refusing her matrimony. I had been turning these thoughts over in my mind while I rode silently by my brother's side.

It was a lovely morning as we rode along the Upper Road on our way to The Hague. The sky was clear blue, the air was hot. So heavenly was the weather that, for a time, I was content with my own thoughts. Black birds, which Jamaicans called Kling-klings, fluttered across the road and lizards lay basking on the rough walls, disappearing on our approach. A thousand sweet scents came out of the pastures and hung in the air. Presently Philip suggested that we should hurry. I was so engrossed with my own speculations that, when I spoke, I forgot he had no clue to my thoughts.

'Do you think he let her go too far?' I asked abruptly.

'Let who go where?'

'Mr Hemans' mistress,' I continued. 'Do you think it was a good thing that, although he let her go so far, he wouldn't let her go as far as she wanted?'

I was worried because, immediately we had begun to trot, Warlock's paces had become uncomfortable. As a four-year-old he had been trained as an ambler (which meant that he trotted with his hind legs and cantered with his fore legs) for this mode of progress had been considered a great accomplishment in his youth. But now, in his old age, he had lost the spring in his joints and continuously threw his rider from side to side as he changed feet to avoid any unevenness in the road.

'Good gracious,' exclaimed Philip, 'what do you know about Mr Hemans' mistress?'

'Nothing,' I replied, 'except what I have been thinking out. But I hoped you might be able to help me.'

When I explained my difficulty, he did try to help me. He did not snub me like other people sometimes did but, to the best of his ability, placed each case before me in simple language which I could understand. While he talked, Mr Hemans and his mistress emerged from the confused position I had imagined them to be in and I began to understand something of the complicated subject of sex and of the rigidity of social laws. He, moreover, said that, since he was only leaving the note and not going into the house, I could accompany him up to The Hague.

The Hague was built on a little hill under which the main road passed. From a distance, looking either back or forward, one could see a line of shuttered windows rising above a stone balustrade. Such houses were rare anywhere in the West Indies where the recurrence of earthquakes and hurricanes discouraged owners of land from building large stone dwellings. There was something distinguished and at the same time lonely about the house and that row of windows. I had never once seen a shutter thrown back or a figure on the terrace, nor had I ever seen a buggy going either up or down the road to the house. Was this air, which the place gave out, of being set apart from the world natural to it or had solitude been forced on it by circumstances?

As my brother and I left the main road and walked our horses up the well-constructed drive to The Hague, I felt pleased, not exactly excited, but intensely interested.

We made a half circle of the hill before turning to the north up a steep, grass slope. In another minute we had passed through an iron gate and were in a grass-covered space enclosed by buildings. To my right was a low verandah approached by stone steps. Before me were outbuildings, probably kitchens, with doors but no windows. On my left, at some distance, were coach houses and stables. All was neat. The only living things I could see were a dog asleep in the sun and a few fowls which lay dusting themselves by the open door of the coach house. No servants came running to greet us and no black heads were thrust out of doorways. I wondered whether all the inhabitants of the place were asleep or whether perhaps they were only so unused to communication with the outer world and resigned to the silence of the long empty days that they had given up hope of anything ever happening.

We drew up. Presently Philip raised his voice and shouted, 'Hoy.' The dog lifted its head, looked at us indifferently and then fell once more into its original posture of complete somnolence. What an odd place this was where even dogs forgot to bark at strangers.

Growing impatient, my brother left my side and, riding up to the flight of steps, shouted, 'Is anyone there?' This I knew to be the correct West Indian greeting, there being no bells to ring or knockers to knock as there are in England. This time a door at the end of the verandah opened and Mr Cameron came out. Seeing the young man for the first time in strange surroundings gave me a sort of shock. He was dressed as he always had been while with us at that hour of the morning. His linen coat and trousers were curiously familiar to me and even his silk shirt and brown leather slippers struck a homely note, but he himself seemed to have gone far away. In a short space of time, twenty-four hours to be exact, he had become another person.

I sat on my horse in the middle of the sun-baked yard and watched the two men greet each other. Philip dismounted and passed over the note which we had brought and then, gathering up his reins, he prepared to mount once more. Having completed what we had come to do, he now considered that he and I might be off about our own business without delay. It seemed as if this strange drowsy place was about to engulf a live friend yet, no more than the dog sleeping in the sun nor the fowls dusting themselves before the open doors of the coach house, did I wish to thrust myself forward to prevent this.

Then, all in a minute, the door at the end of the verandah was flung open once more and Mr Hemans came bustling out. At one and the same time he waved to me, greeted Philip and shouted to some far unseen 'boy' to come and take our horses. Having broken the heavy silence, he called into the recesses of the house for drinks. He made me feel as if someone were trying to wake me from a midday slumber and was only being partially successful. 'Come on! Come on!' he shouted, 'you must certainly get off.' While speaking, he hurried along the verandah and down the steps as quickly as his weight and the heelless slippers he wore would allow him. Evidently he intended to drag me from my horse by force, if necessary, but, at the foot of the steps, Philip laid a hand on his arm and said in a determined voice, 'No. She cannot come in.'

This remark, though outspoken, might not have discouraged our would-be host had not two females come out at this moment by the same door through which he had made his exit and stood on the verandah looking down on us smilingly. They were both black and, though apparently uncertain of their welcome, were most decidedly determined to stay and look at me. Their inopportune arrival brought Mr Hemans to a standstill. He hesitated, then, turning and hurrying up the steps, he waved his arms at them, ordering them to retire back into the house. This, however, they did not do. They continued to smile and look down unperturbed. I felt uncomfortable. Mr Hemans' efforts and frustration were like an odd personal play which was being acted out and which was, in some way, personally related to me and my feelings.

Having failed to drive these members of his household away, Mr Hemans, for the third time, bustled along the verandah, but before he was able to descend, Philip, who had remained standing at the foot of the steps with his pony's reins in his hands, barred his way, and bringing him to a halt, held him in conversation.

While they talked, Mr Cameron drifted slowly towards me. With each step he took he became a little more real until, as he put out his hand to touch Warlock, he himself had once more occupied his familiar clothes. Even though he did not speak to me, his presence was a comfort and a sort of protection. The other people present seemed so busy, each in his or her own way, that it did not seem necessary for either Mr Cameron or me to make the least effort.

Philip was now arguing loudly with Mr Hemans and I knew by the tone of his voice that, in spite of Mr Hemans' insistence, my brother was going to win and that I would not be allowed to dismount and go into the house.

It is not easy to describe a scene of which, at the time, I was only half conscious. That yard had made me feel as sleepy as the dog and the fowls. When Philip parted from Mr Hemans, I woke up with a start for his last remark – 'You can't have your cake and eat it' – sounded so like a nursery rhyme that I couldn't help feeling sorry for the fat man. He looked so dejected and limp that I was only able to reply half-heartedly to the vociferous goodbyes of the two women who were now leaning over the verandah railings to see us ride away.

At the very last possible moment, Mr Cameron pulled a letter out of his shirt front and handed it to me. Thinking that this must be a letter to my mother, I took it from him and, slipping it into my jacket pocket, said politely, 'Thank you. I will give it to my mother.'

But, when we were a little distance from the house, Philip turned to me and asked, 'Did Mr Cameron give you a letter?'

The moment he spoke I felt there was something odd about that letter. It was not just an ordinary answer to an invitation to tea or dinner. In any case, I now realised that Mr Cameron must have written it before we got to The Hague.

Slipping my hand into my jacket pocket I withdrew the envelope far enough to read what was written on it. To my surprise, I found that it was addressed to me.

'It's to me,' I said apologetically.

'Well, wait a minute,' said Philip.

On the main road he took my reins and I opened and read the letter. Gradually my brother's pony pushed Warlock until he was on the rough grass at the side of the road. For fear of being observed by anyone who might be peeping through the shuttered windows high above us, we did not pull up the horses but continued at a canter. And there, being jerked to and fro by Warlock and occasionally heaved up unexpectedly over a drain, I read my first proposal of marriage.

From the bottom of my heart I wished Mr Cameron had not written that letter. It was not a bit what I had imagined a proposal would be. In fact it was more a series of reprimands and a declaration of unwilling affection than a love letter.

When I had finished reading it, I passed the missive shamefacedly to my brother. Was I really what Mr Cameron said I was and was he justified in being angry with me? Of course I had admired his riding and been pleased when he had stayed with Alice Reay and me when he might so easily have avoided us. But had I really, as he said, lured him on and dragged him, all unwilling, into this state of mind which he called love?

While Philip read, I gathered up my reins but I did not resume control of Warlock. He and I were out of touch with each other. All in a minute I felt dreadfully hurt. My idea of love was a very different thing. It was bright and gentle and all mixed up with dreams and colours and understanding people. Mr Cameron must have been mistaken. Real love could not possibly hurt another person on such a beautiful day as this. Hot, burning tears jumped out of my eyes and they did not do me a bit of good.

All along the Upper Road, Warlock galloped with my brother's pony pounding behind him. At the front steps of Arcadia, I pulled myself together to take my letter and give up my horse. Then I ran through the house and upstairs to my mother's room. She was sitting in front of her looking glass brushing the front of her hair and putting on her rings. I handed her my letter.

To me, it seemed a long while before she finished reading but, in the end, she folded it carefully and put it into a little drawer by her looking glass.

'You will have to answer that,' she said and added in a worried voice, 'but don't tell your father.'

I had not thought of telling my father but I did not say

so. Later that day I wrote a note to Mr Cameron in which I said I was sorry but that I was only sixteen and that, when I returned to England, I should be going to school. Letters were always a difficulty to me. As a rule mother would tell me that I could make more of what I had to say. This time, however, she did not make any suggestions so my reply to Mr Cameron went as it was.

For weeks after I felt uncomfortable when anyone mentioned his name but, in the end, as the others did, I seemed to forget all about him.

CHAPTER 11

The Green Iguana

TWO BIG IGUANA LIZARDS lived in the fig tree by the wood stack at Arcadia. It was great fun to climb onto the wood and stare up into the branches until the lizards appeared. They could change their colour and make themselves look exactly like anything on which they happened to be sitting so, for a time, even though one knew perfectly well that they must be in the tree, one could not see them.

In the end, if you stood perfectly quiet and did not allow the wood to rattle, one of the lizards would give himself away. An orange bag would come out under his chin and then you could see his glittering eyes and trace the lovely long line of his back and tail. Against the smooth, olive-green bark of the fig tree, the lizards looked opaque and dull but I always thought that they liked to be bright green and iridescent best.

One morning, I was sitting on the verandah with a lighted candle on the table beside me, picking ticks off my dog Bundle. He was lying on his back with his four feet in the air and a sentimental expression on his face and, by this, I knew that, even though the operation pleased him, he was not sure if it were right for a house dog to have ticks at all. I had caught the hundredth and put it in the candle flame where it exploded with a pop and an unpleasant smell. At the east end of the verandah my father paced to and fro. My mother was downstairs superintending the making of preserved limes. Where Beattie was, for once, I did not know.

For me this was the quiet time of the early morning. Bundle and I had had our walk and I was now waiting for the big cans of hot and cold bath water which would shortly appear up the outside iron staircase, preceded by Princess' black, curled head and sulky face.

For the moment, I had nothing to do and little to occupy my mind. The regular appearance and disappearance of my father soothed me and carried my thoughts away. He was still in his white cotton pyjama coat and had tucked his trousers into a pair of socks. On his head he wore a Neapolitan sailor's cap, carrying under his arm a brass spy glass and on his feet were his red heelless slippers. Dressed as he was, he brought back to my mind a story I had read as a child. He might well have been the pirate – the grim hero of the tale – for, although I knew perfectly well that the spy glass was to be focused on nothing more important than a rum coaster beating up against the trade wind along the north coast of Jamaica, it pleased me to imagine that we were sailing the Caribbean Sea in search of a rich prize and that the spy glass might as easily pick up a fully rigged ship bound for Spain with a cargo of gold and spices.

I was roused from my daydream by a call from my father, so blowing out the candle and pushing Bundle through the gate of the outside staircase, I ran along to the east end of the verandah.

There I found him looking down into the little enclosed garden at that side of the house. I joined him at the rail and peeped over. Below me was a square garden surrounded by iron railings. In it were red and yellow coloas and rose trees, each in a little round bed of its own. A hen and her family of chicks had been put in there for safety's sake by

Mary the cook and I could see the chicks in a group in the sunlight but they had been disturbed.

'What is it?' I asked my father.

'Look,' he said, pointing to a shadow.

There, under one of the coloas, was the biggest of my iguana lizards and, in front of him, stood the mother hen. My lizard had evidently seen the chickens from his home in the fig tree and had come over to see what he could get in the way of a meal. The hen, however, was determined to do her best to protect her young. She ruffled up her feathers and went bravely into battle.

For a time I was interested in what was going on below me, then it dawned on me that this fight had to be to the finish. Either the hen or the big lizard would win and the loser would have to die. There would be no quarter and I was afraid for the lizard.

'May I go down and stop them?' I asked suddenly.

'No,' replied my father. 'This is interesting. I have never seen a fight between a hen and one of your lizards. I want to see which one will win.'

The hen made little rushes. The lizard jumped right off the ground. Sometimes the hen lost a tuft of feathers which floated away on the air and, once, the lizard caught her by the leg and made her squawk; but, more often, her vicious pecks landed on his body or tail.

The old hen did not endear herself to me by her tactics. She was spiteful and, when it seemed that her opponent would willingly have escaped, she would not allow him to do so and always managed to put herself between him and the railings. There was a horrible lust in her actions and her yellow eyes gleamed.

'Which do you think will win?' I asked my father.

'Can't say. They are both good fighters.'

'Then may I stop them?' I begged.

My father took his eyes off the fight and looked at me, so what I said must have surprised him. 'Why do you want to stop them?' he asked.

'Because I think the hen will win.'

'Well, so do I, but that is no reason.'

'Well ... because I like the lizard.'

'How can you like a reptile?'

'I like him because he is beautiful,' I said shamefacedly.

I had thought that only snakes and crocodiles were reptiles and was sorry to hear that a creature that could turn such beautiful colours could be one also. I knew I should never climb up onto the wood pile again and watch the two iguanas thrust out their orange bags to attract the flies and flicker their eyes and change colour when the sun came through the leaves to make bright patches on the smooth bark of the fig tree.

I wanted to go away but something forced me to stay and see the end. It was not long in coming. Before the lizard died, he went through the colours of the rainbow and then a light seemed to go out inside him and he turned a leaden colour. After that the hen tore him to shreds and ate him.

It seemed hard that one creature should have to die because it had made a mistake and come down out of its tree, but harder still that an unattractive hen should have put out such a beautiful light.

CHAPTER 12

The Dance

WHEN WE REACHED RETREAT, where the dance was to be held, other buggies were driving up and I saw two or three parties get out and disappear into the house. When our turn came I followed Mother and Beattie up the steps.

In front of us, on a table, was a big plate covered with programmes. The little cards had coloured pictures on them and pencils hung down all round. Some of these were pink and some blue.

On the left was a room so full of coats and shoes that they overflowed onto the verandah. A young man was picking these up and pushing them back into the room. I soon saw that we should have to pass through the ballroom before we could take off our wraps and I felt ashamed because I had woolly shoes on over my satin slippers.

Young people were standing about in the dancing room looking self-conscious and near the piano there were three musicians getting ready to play.

A terrific excitement began to bubble up inside me. So overpowering was this feeling that Mother had to push me into the ladies' dressing room and take my cloak from me. I felt obstinate and helpless and did not want to look at myself in the mirror but turned my head to one side when Beattie made room for me in front of the dressing-table. There were eight or nine girls in the room and some older people, all of whom my mother greeted. Three of the girls I noticed because they were pretty and seemed interested in us. The eldest was dark and small, the second had hair drawn right back from her face which, in spite of this severe style, was calm and lovely, the third, who was fair too, was even younger than I was. Their mother and my mother began to talk to each other in a pleasant and amused way, but we girls stared at each other in silence. I could hear my mother saying, 'Yes, my younger daughter is not out yet either.' And the other mother replied, 'I ought not to have brought Rene but she was so disappointed that she … '

What Rene had done to persuade her mother to bring her to the dance dwindled into silence as we all walked out into the ballroom. Then Mother made a sign to Beattie and me to follow and I knew that the moment had come for us to remember our manners. I must neither speak to nor smile at anyone, even the people with whom I was acquainted, until we had greeted our hostess who was Alice Reay dressed in black lace. This my Mother called 'deportment' and she had reminded me before we had left home that anyone could tell a well-brought-up girl by the way she walked into a ballroom. When my turn came I shook hands with Alice and said, 'How do you do?' and Alice said to me, 'I am glad you have come.'

This evidently fulfilled the correct code of manners for a lot of young men then came up and asked us to dance. Bill gave me a programme which he had been trying to push into my hand ever since we had come into the room but which I had refused to notice on account of manners and our not having said 'How do you do?' to our hostess.

Then, all in a minute, I was in a whirl and very happy. The music began. I danced a waltz and a polka and another waltz. This was spelt 'Valse' on my programme. Nearly all the men had on white kid gloves and were dressed in evening suits and white waistcoats; but a few had short jackets and wore black ties. They all looked happy and earnest and some of the younger ones counted 'one, two, three,' as they danced.

When the first confusion was over I noticed that the musicians were foreigners and that they watched us as we danced. One of the girls we had met in the ladies dressing room (the slight, dark one) went up to them in the interval and spoke to them. I heard someone say they were Italians and that she had been in Italy. The three musicians looked pleased at this attention and stood up and bowed to her when she had finished speaking and her partner came to claim her. I wished I had been able to speak Italian also, although, even had I been able to do so, I would not have had sufficient courage to walk up to those men before so many strangers.

While we were dancing the floor was packed, but when we stopped, I recognised the room as the one where we had played games on the day of the polo match. It was quite changed because everything had been taken out of it except the clock and that had stopped at 3.15. A lot of people asked me to dance and put their names on my programme which I handed to them. But Bill said, 'You don't want all those partners.'

'Why not?' I asked

'Because it is better to dance with only a few and get to know their steps.'

I thought it would take a long time to get used to Bill's steps as, even though he played polo so well and I was proud to be with him, he could not dance well and had to count all the time. However, to have said I rather liked a change would have been impolite and, as a lot of other dancers jostled us and bumped us while we were dancing, I only remarked, 'Isn't this rather like riding people off at polo?' and Bill was pleased.

After a time, it grew hot and we drank lime juice and fanned ourselves with palm leaves which Alice had hung round the room. Bill suggested I should go into supper with him, but I said this was impossible as someone else had written his name on my programme over the three little dances called supper extras. We spent some time trying to read his name and, when the young man eventually came up, Bill said, 'Oh him,' in such a voice that I felt only continuous courtesy could put things right.

At supper, I sat opposite the second of the three sisters and I thought she looked more beautiful than ever. She and her partner did not speak to each other and I do not believe they ate much. They seemed to me to be shut away together and to be unaware of the talk and laughter going on round them.

There were dishes of sandwiches on the tables and these were passed up and down from hand to hand. One could not tell what they were made of until one bit into one and then it was too late to put it down or to have another if it happened to be nice. In front of me were oranges which had been filled with jelly. I wondered why we did not have such things at home. My partner told me that his sister had made them and that she had been afraid they would not set. Partly out of politeness and partly because I really liked them, I ate two.

The girls at the dance were well dressed but I thought my sister was the most magnificent of all. She was wearing the dress which had been made in England and which she had worn for the first time at the ball in Kingston. The skirt was made of blue moiré and the bodice and sleeves were of tucked chiffon of the same colour and the whole effect was lovely. My frock was much simpler. It was made of white crepon which had a satin rib running through it and round the neck the dressmaker had arranged a white chiffon frill caught up on the shoulders by bunches of imitation daisies. These daisies, being untropical, pleased my partners, many of whom told me that they suited me. After supper I discovered I had lost my programme. The little book was no longer hanging on my wrist and there was no sign of it when the room cleared after we had danced the last of the supper extras. Knowing that it had been filled within a few minutes of my arrival, I did not, at first, think my loss was important, but when no one came to claim the next dance or the one after that, I felt worried.

'Why are you not dancing?' asked Beattie as she passed on her way out of the room.

'I've lost my programme,' I answered somewhat morosely for I felt that I was not, after all, a genuine wallflower.

'Well then, take anybody,' she said, and in a moment she had gone, leaving me alone once more.

It was all very well for her to say, 'Take anybody,' but how could I take a fresh partner if no one presented himself. I glanced towards the doorway where several young men were grouped but among them I saw no one I knew well and those who came in and out during the intervals were evidently hunting for their rightful partners.

When the music once more struck up, Alice Reay noticed me and came quickly across to me.

'Oh never mind your programme,' she said in answer to my explanation. 'I will get you another. There are heaps of boys who want to dance.'

But to my horror, the first two whom she spoke to looked at me and shook their heads. They evidently did not wish to dance. When Alice eventually came back, she brought with her a tall thin young man whom I had never seen before. He was a stranger and, to my relief, seemed pleased to find anyone willing to dance with him. So we took our places for a lancers which was being got up.

At one end of the room a stage had been built where mothers could sit in a row and watch the dancers. Long before this, all the mothers had climbed down from the stage by a little ladder in the middle and walked away together to the supper room. Now, deprived of their restraining influence, the young men became noisy. They took hands and galloped round and, in the middle of one of these twirls, I looked up and caught a glimpse of Bill. He was standing by the further doorway which led out onto the verandah and was watching us intently. He was, as far as I could see, incredibly untidy. His shirt front was ripped open from neck to waist, his collar was unbuttoned and his dark hair was on end. However, when I was able to look towards the doorway again, he had disappeared and his place had been taken by a black manservant bearing a tray with glasses. Perhaps I was thinking more of his appearance than of my steps for, when my partner pulled me roughly back, I struck my heels against the lowest rung of the ladder which led up onto the stage and I sat down on it. Had I only sat on the steps it would not have mattered very much but I upset a pot plant which had been placed there as an ornament and it fell onto its side and, getting under my knees, it ran with me into the middle of the floor. At this, there was a roar of laughter and the music stopped.

I scrambled quickly to my feet and someone came and carried the plant away, but I felt indignant and ashamed and, as soon as I was able to escape, I left the dance floor and went out onto the verandah. It was lovely and cool outside. The moon was covered by a small cloud but it was shining in a sky which was glittering as if it were made of silver spangles. One or two couples were standing about. I avoided them and jumped down into the garden. Soon a big oleander bush hid me from the house and I stood there thinking how lovely the night was and how I should like to forget where I was.

When the moon came out from behind the cloud I put my face close to the oleander blossoms which were sweet and cool. They made me forget that I had, only a few minutes before, felt upset over my clumsy action in the ballroom and soon I was happy and excited because rays of light seemed to come out of the flowers and my thoughts went back into my mind as they do in dreams.

Presently, however, I found that I was not alone. Two people, a man and a girl, were standing by a hedge not far from the bush which sheltered me. I think the reason I had not seen them at once was that he was dressed in black and she in white and the hedge was black and white-black in shadow and white where the moonlight fell. Many points of light twinkled in the hedge and when I put my hand out and touched them, I found that they were dew drops.

The man and the girl did not move and soon I forgot to be afraid that they might see me. She was the second of the three sisters whom I had seen in the dressing room and he was the man who had been her partner at the supper table. They were so engrossed in each other that they made me feel as if I were part of a dream and not a real person at all.

When they went back into the dance room, I picked a piece of the hedge and with it in my hand climbed onto the stage where my mother was now sitting.

Presently Bill, who had changed into a clean shirt and collar, came and asked me where I had been hiding. I did not tell him.

Ages after, when we were driving home, I heard my mother say to Beattie, 'I understand that the second Miss Fletcher is engaged to young Frank Kelly. It is a bright future for her.'

But how bright it was I did not believe that even my mother could know.

CHAPTER 13

Bill

'I AM VERY SORRY,' said Bill.

He and I were standing on the verandah at Arcadia looking out to the north. It was early on the afternoon of the day following the dance and he was dressed in his Sunday suit.

'I really am sorry,' he repeated, continuing to gaze, not at me, but out over the sea. 'And I have come, with my brother, to apologise.'

As I did not reply, the worried expression on his face deepened.

'Will you forgive me?' he pleaded.

Avoiding a direct answer I began to question him as to what had happened on the previous evening. 'Do you mean to say that you actually fought and prevented my partners coming to dance with me?'

'Yes I did.'

'How many of them?'

'Four, I think.'

Bill was physically strong and in hard condition and I could imagine that what he said was no more than the truth. The recollection of the untidy figure he had cut in the doorway at Retreat the previous evening came back to me, reminding me that he would be well able to fight and win if he set his mind to it. But that he should have wanted anything sufficiently to make him forget the ordinary courtesy which he owed to his guests staggered me. I felt as if I were up against something elemental and uncontrolled in him, something which I had never met with before and which I found it difficult to understand.

Being uncertain how to cope with the situation and a little puzzled by Bill's manner, I fell back on the admonition I myself had so often received when I had done anything wrong in the school room.

'Do you think that was kind?'

Bill changed his weight from one foot to the other. He seemed uncomfortable.

'I didn't hurt any of them,' he said quickly, 'at least not seriously. Most of them were quite willing to give you up when they saw I was earnest.'

'I have no doubt of that.'

My answer was, I thought, a smart and clever one; but my sarcasm was lost on my companion. His hair was unusually well brushed, probably thanks to his brother's good offices. His merry face was drawn into serious lines but he did not seem really upset. There was no sign in his face or manner that he regretted what he had done.

'When I said "was it kind?" I did not mean "did you hurt them?"' I said. 'But was it kind of you, as a host, to treat your guests like that?'

Bill answered in his usual calm, unruffled voice.

'No, it was not. That is what my brother said and that is why I have come to apologise.'

I found it difficult to argue successfully with anyone who agreed with me and yet who refused to look at me. As far as I could see, he had been told what to say to me and had learnt his lesson well. I could imagine his elder brother insisting that he should come and apologise, rubbing in the enormity of his deed on the long drive from Retreat. But had Bill really been wrong to fight those young men?

'Why did you do it?' I asked suddenly.

Bill made no reply to this. He simply continued to stare obstinately at the sea.

'Aren't you going to tell me?' I pleaded.

'No.'

'Then what in the world was the good of your coming here to say you are sorry, when you won't tell me why and when you knew perfectly well that you don't regret anything?'

This was evidently an entirely new point of view to Bill and it was also not what he had expected me to say so I took advantage of his confusion to drive home my advantage.

'And was it kind to me?'

'To you ... I don't understand?'

It was quite obvious that this was true. Bill did not understand. He had been so full of his own thoughts and so determined that he had indeed been really and truly right in what he had done that my question took him unawares.

'Well, you must see that you rather spoilt the dance for me,' I said, trying by repetition to drive my point home.

Bill's answer startled me.

'You know I wouldn't hurt you for the world.'

He was now so very much in earnest and the pain in his voice was so clear that he made me feel small-minded and ashamed of having brought myself into the conversation at all. It was as if I, for my own ends, had been trying to bully a child into saying why he was sorry.

'How did I spoil the dance for you?' he repeated. 'Unless, of course, you wanted to dance with any of those blighters. Did you?'

'No. Not particularly.'

Here I simply had to smile in spite of my determination to keep serious. Bill was not one of those 'dog in the manger' sort of people who would try to prevent another person from getting what he himself might want so he must have had some other reason for preventing my partners from dancing with me. Of this I was convinced. Maybe one of them had said something he did not like, maybe another might have thought it fine and manly to boast of his success with girls. I know things like that were said; and thoughts like that were unfortunately common; but I also knew that, although Bill was simple-minded, he could, at times, be obstinate. I should never hear anything ugly from him. Still, because he had not chosen to tell me what was in his mind when I asked him, I (childlike) determined to tease him.

'Thank you so much for telling me,' I said lightly. 'I am glad to know what they said.'

At this Bill's whole expression altered. I had never known him so nearly furious.

'You don't know, and you never will hear from me,' he vociferated angrily.

And then our talk, or as much of it as is interesting, ended.

But later I thought to myself that I did know, and that he had told me a great deal more of himself and of others than he knew.

CHAPTER 14

Oxford (2)

A FORTNIGHT AFTER the dance I got my wish: the hoped-for visit to Oxford came to pass. My memory of Jamaica has one peculiarity that is not equalled by impressions from elsewhere. Each event, as it returns in my memory, brings with it some of the original feelings of expectancy and surprise and even the places share in this delightful freshness. As we, Beattie and I, rode into Oxford yard (on this second occasion) with the certainty in our hearts that we were to enjoy to the full the out-of-door life, I felt sure of myself. Arcadia was all make-believe, a tiresome imitation of English life. This was going to be the real thing at last.

The sun was hot, much hotter than it had been on our previous visits. Everything seemed to sparkle and snap. The little hills were jumping and the big ones nodding in the haze. We had no bundles strapped to our saddles. A real trunk was to come over later in the double buggy. We rode because that seemed the easiest manner to take over our horses, which we would need on the sugar estate.

As we trotted into the yard I pushed Victoria up to the wall of the cattle pen and, raising myself in my stirrups, peeped over. There were quite a lot of cattle inside the pen.

'What is the name of that one?' I asked a young black Jamaican who was chewing a piece of cane.

He rose and came towards me.

'Me Sammy Two, Oxford cattle boy,' he said with a wide grin. 'Dat dar steer am Rajah, young Misses.'

I nodded.

'And that one?'

'And that ... and that ... ?'

'Mal'vil, Mo'batten, Nelson, Blake ... '

When he had named about fifteen I stopped him. 'Funny names aren't they?' I said.

'Berry funny! young Misses,' but he looked at me as if he thought I was funnier than the names.

'Who names them?'

'Me no know, young Misses. All named by cattlemen when little baby calf up in de hills.'

I thought of the cattle count and of the headman who had called out all the names, and asked no more questions. 'Well, thank you Sammy, and goodbye,' I said, pulling Victoria round.

'Tank you Misses. All berry pleased to see young Misses at Oxford.'

We received the same sort of friendly greeting all over the estate. It made me feel very happy. That afternoon we were shown over the boiler house and still houses. We saw sugar manufacturing in all its phases, from the big coppers where the juice was boiled to the upper room where the finished sugar came out golden and dry from the centrifuges.

Later in the same afternoon we rode to see Philip inspect a guinea grass pasture which was being cleaned and watched him measure the amount of land each man had cleared. As we came back through the yard on our way home, I stopped again to ask Sammy Two for another fifteen or so names.

This went on for four days. After the first day, I had to write these names on strips of paper which I carried about in my coat pocket and, each night before going to bed, I leant out of the Busha House window and, staring into the black darkness, repeated the names of the steers which I had learnt. With each whispered repetition of Busha, Melville, Mountbatten, Blake or Nelson I saw a steer. One had a black patch, one had a broken horn, one was all black, one was all white. Each had some distinctive feature which made him stand out from his fellows.

In this manner the days passed pleasantly. On Friday, Philip said to me, 'You can come with me and count the canes. Beattie can go through the pic'ny gang book while we are away. Tomorrow is pay day. No one works on Saturday.'

'Don't they?' I queried.

'No, the estate workers nearly all have land in the hills and, on Saturday, they go up there and plant or bring back yams and other vegetables which they have grown. Some of them go a long distance.'

I was in such a hurry to go with my brother to count canes that I hardly ate any lunch and, in the end, I was waiting outside long before he was ready.

The cane piece which was being cut was some distance away and we rode there, but every yard of the way was pure joy. Kling-klings were singing in the hollows, lizards were basking on the rough stone walls and, when I screwed up my eyes to look into the sky, I could see the John Crows sailing far overhead. They looked beautiful but I knew that, close at hand with their scrawny necks and red heads, they were anything but beautiful and the knowledge that they were there looking on gave me a feeling of insecurity.

'If I died,' I said to my brother, 'how long would it take for a John Crow to come?'

'No time at all. They have wonderful sight. That one up

there would come at once and the next one would see him drop and fly over to find out what was wrong and the next and the next would follow suit. In a few minutes you would have twenty or thirty of them perched round you.'

'How gruesome,' I said, feeling uncomfortable.

'Not at all, in a hot climate like this,' Philip said. 'It is a good thing as we don't have to bury our stock.'

'And what about humans?' I suggested, glancing at the big bird balancing itself easily on outspread wings in the glittering sky.

'Oh, we don't leave each other to the John Crows. We keep our own planks for emergencies.'

'Planks!' said I, my thoughts flying to rafts and an unpremeditated embarkation on the beautiful tropical sea. And then, as the truth sank into my mind, 'Oh, you mean coffins.'

'Yes, stupid! What else should I mean? Mine are in the store room, under the drawing room at the Busha House.'

Short of choosing the name plate and handles, there did not seem to be anything further to discuss, so I rode on in silence. Death, which a few minutes before had seemed so far from my brother and me had, during our conversation, crept close enough to peep at us from behind stone walls and to stare out of the ponds in the hollows.

When we reached the cane field, Philip dismounted and gave his horse to a boy to hold. 'Come on,' he said to me. 'I'll give you something better to think about than death and destruction!'

I did as he said and was soon following him on foot through the thick cane litter scattered over the field. There were eight cutters, seven men and one woman – all armed with machetes and dressed in every sort of rag to protect them from the sharp-edged leaves of the canes. These people looked at me with interest. I do not suppose they often saw an English girl (or, as they would have said, 'a buckra woman') in the fields and they all greeted me with expressions of delight.

'Alexandra,' said my brother, walking up to one of them, 'I have brought my sister to count your canes so mind you have them right.'

This sally was received with roars of laughter. Alexandra, placing her hands on her enormous hips, opened her mouth to its widest, thus displaying a lovely set of teeth and a very red tongue. She did not speak but treated my brother to the coyest of glances and, after each look, broke into fresh peals of laughter.

'Come on,' said Philip, taking me by the elbow and drawing me to a pile of cut canes. 'Alexandra will like to have her canes counted by you! But remember, she is the best dissembler on the property, so catch her out. I never can.'

With his foot he touched the first pile. 'Now each bundle is supposed, I say supposed' – this with a mock serious glance at Alexandra – 'to contain twelve sticks and each pile twelve bundles. You can pick one bundle to count or one pile if you think it may be short of the correct number. If you are right the cutter loses payment for that pile. But if you are wrong you can't count another. These are the rules of the game, so go ahead.'

I looked shyly at the circle of smiling faces and then at the heap of canes in front of me. Alexandra's personality oppressed me. She would not, I thought, be obvious. So this bundle at my feet with a particularly large sugar cane and several small ones in it would probably be correct and placed there to catch my eye. On the other hand, that other one at the side composed of medium sized canes might be short and then, again, it might not. Lying as they did all heaped together it was impossible to get more than a general impression of how many canes each contained. 'I'll count a bundle,' I whispered to Philip.

'All right, fire away.'

'That one,' I said stretching out my hand. At the last second I had changed my mind and chosen one at the far side of the heap. It was loosely tied. Also, while I hesitated, Alexandra had stopped laughing and looked – or I fancied she had looked – in that direction. Anyhow I took a risk.

'That one?' asked Philip briskly.

'Yes.'

'Well, count that one, Alexandra, and we shall see.'

With a typical roll of her hips the big negress launched herself at the heaps of canes, abstracted the bundle I had pointed out and, unfastening it, laid the contents at our feet.

'One, two, three, four ... ' counted Philip and then, suddenly, 'Caught at last. That will make up for a few of the times you have taken me in, Alexandra.'

I was not so successful with the other cutters but Philip, who took over from me for the last two, docked them each of one pile.

'Do they always do that?' I asked, as I once more followed him to the place where our ponies were waiting for us.

'Yes, always, but I'm glad you caught Alexandra. She makes more money than any of the others. What made you pick that particular bundle; was it just chance?'

'Not altogether.' I pushed Victoria up to the wall and climbed into the saddle. 'I didn't really like her character so that made it easy.'

Philip stopped to settle his stirrup leathers.

'Oh, did it?' he said thoughtfully. 'So you find your theory applies to Jamaicans as well?'

'Of course.'

'Then what were they all?'

'The others were probably pleasing like you, or combined. She was animal-suave, and I don't very much like animal-suave when they are like that.'

'Do you know why?'

'No,' I said, but in my heart I felt that I ought to have known why I had not liked her.

We rode on to the next field where the same amusing game of catch-who-catch-can took place. But here all the cutters were men and, to my mind, they were pleasanter to deal with than Alexandra had been. Each had one or two helpers with him and these added to the fun and the jokes which were bandied to and fro and which were renewed at each success or failure on my part. Just as we finished, the bullock wagons came down the road and turned into the field to clear away the last of the cut canes. By this time I knew the waggoners by name and the cattle too and, with the intention of renewing what was so bright and clear in my mind and of finally driving the last thought of Alexandra out of my head, I waited to see the laden wagons draw out of the field. Yes, there in the first team were Melville and Blake in the lead, with two young steers next, and on either side of the pole two more quiet, reliable animals. It was, I suppose, what might have been called a well-balanced team but the quick feeling of delight I experienced on seeing them was caused more by the fact that I had recognised each straining bullock than by the consideration of their perfection as a whole.

After the first wagon had passed, I turned my head to look at the next one which was just approaching the gap in

The voyage out

The ship's doctor

The captain

A woman near Arcadia

Arcadia (from the flagpole)

Arcadia: balustrade and flagpole overlooking sea and Cuba

Left: Me
Below left: Me with Bundle
Below right: Jack

Me on Coquette

Left: Me playing tennis
Below: Just off to the dance

Mahogany Hall

Mahogany Hall: Beattie, Me, Catherine & Lucy Locket

Swimming: Harmony Hall wharf

Harmony Hall wharf

the wall through which it also had to pass. I suppose the waggoner saw me turn my head for he began to crack his whip and to halloo and, as the six animals went running past, I noticed two things. One was that the driver did not call out the names of his cattle as drivers generally did when encouraging them to pull their hardest and, two, that one of his team had been out on the previous day! As soon as the wagon had cleared the gap, I motioned to him to stop.

'You had that third steer on the right out yesterday,' I said to the big, barefooted man who came up to me. 'See it doesn't happen again.'

The look of surprise on his face was ludicrous. I could see the whites of his staring eyes and the crestfallen expression on his face.

'Young Misses perfec'ly right. Me no use dat steer anny mo,' was all he said but I had much ado not to join in the shouts of amusement and delight which the other drivers indulged in. They were overjoyed at their comrade's discomfiture. One doubled up, completely overcome with merriment, while another cried out witticisms which I was not able to understand but which were obvious in their intention. The last driver, evidently sure of his team, struck his leader a resounding blow with the flat of his hand, apostrophising it with the remark, 'Get 'long wid yo, Busha. Doan yo know what wark is?'

I knew this was meant as a reference to my brother who had joined me and who remained unmoved, this being a well-worn joke and one which he was evidently used to. My detection of the steer which had been worked two days running was quite another matter and it evidently pleased him. 'They'll never forget that,' he said as we followed the wagons down the road. 'And how you did it in so short a time I don't know. It takes these Jamaicans weeks to learn the names of a herd and they are with them all day long. And some of my field bookkeepers never learn them all.'

All of my uncomfortable feelings regarding Alexandra were now banished. I felt perfectly and completely certain that this was the life for me and Jamaica a lovely place to live in. However, this contentment was short-lived for, in order to reach the works, we had, once again, to pass the field where we had counted canes earlier in the afternoon. There we found a single buggy drawn up by the side of the road and by it stood Alexandra. I was about to ride past but Philip had a social sense and, as he either recognised the buggy and horses, or at any rate felt that they should be familiar to him, he pulled up and a shout from under the hood proved that he was correct for it was Herr Bauer who climbed out.

Of course I had seen Herr Bauer many times since I had paid my first visit to the office with my father but I had been able to avoid any considerable conversation with him. Lately a semi-neutrality had taken the place of our open antagonism. During the winter, he had suggested that I should buy a Kodak and had offered to order one for me from a store in New York. Although this purchase was to be made with my own money which was administered by the office staff, his suggestion was obviously a bribe and, against my better judgement, I agreed to it. Had he selected anything else for me to buy, I should have had no difficulty in refusing but a Kodak was what I had been longing for and, as no one seemed likely to give me one and as my father never suggested I should buy anything for myself, I gave in and the Kodak was ordered.

When it came, I was pleased. I took a lot of photographs and modified my ungracious behaviour to Herr Bauer. After all, I thought, my opinion of him was based on surmise and suspicion. The Kodak was a fact. However, in the spring, I left the Kodak in the sun and the oblong wooden box in which it was made warped. Immediately all my dislikes of Herr Bauer returned and I felt relieved of my unwilling gratitude to him. My mental attitude was, I knew, perfectly unreasonable but I could not avoid it.

When Herr Bauer climbed out of the buggy on that afternoon, he seemed annoyed at meeting us. Walking up to my brother he hardly greeted him and then began to mention all sorts of mistakes in the management of the estate which Philip was supposed to have made. I was so startled by his flow of sarcastic and abusive remarks that, for a minute or two, I was unable to think or feel anything but a desire to escape. Then, suddenly, a movement on the part of Alexandra attracted my attention and made me wonder about the nature of her relationship with Herr Bauer.

Without stopping to think what I was about to do, I slipped off my pony and walked up to my father's attorney.

It did not take long, and I did not speak loudly, but I was trembling with rage and excitement before I had finished. I began: 'You are ... ' and, although I cannot remember what I said, I meant every word of it and, may I be forgiven, I even mentioned Alexandra's children which I guessed were Herr Bauer's.

When I had finished Alexandra cried out and went off down the road in a great hurry. Herr Bauer and I looked at each other in silence, then he climbed back into his buggy and motioned to his boy to drive away.

Philip and I rode home in silence. I could not speak. My teeth were chattering. The setting sun burnt my cold face and hands. Philip's silence and the drawn expression on his face made me feel frightened. And when natural revulsion set in and I began to wonder miserably which of us, my brother or me, had felt the greater surprise at my outburst, I wished I might be dead.

Dinner at Oxford was a silent meal that night. Beattie must have guessed that something was wrong for I saw her glance at Philip and then at me. But the meal ended without any direct question having been put to him or any explanation given by either of us. Surely, I felt, the kindest and most sympathetic people in the world are those who do not enter uninvited into the miseries of others.

We had no rugs at Oxford and only one blanket each on our beds so I took the mat off the floor and, perching myself on the uncomfortable sofa, wrapped it round my shoulders. And, presently, the slow roll of the rocking chairs on which my brother and sister were sitting and the monotonous sound of their voices soothed me into an exhausted sleep.

CHAPTER 15

Sunday in Arcadia

THE DAY AFTER we went back to Arcadia, a Sunday, only four people came to lunch but many more drove up during the afternoon.

When we got up from the lunch table, Beattie went into the morning room, opened the piano and soon we were all singing hymns. Before long every seat in the room was filled and the latecomers said they had heard us singing from a long way away. Everyone seemed happy and contented and only the elderly remained in the porch to smoke cigars.

Of course, Bill and his brother were there and Mr Hemans. All the polo players had come and also nearly all the young men we had met at the Retreat dance. I knew which were Bill's favourite hymns and turned the pages of the book on the piano as a hint to Beattie.

My mother sat on the sofa under the window and my father paced to and fro, up and down the passage before the open door with his hands clasped behind his back. It was my mother who liked us to sing hymns on Sunday afternoons and she asked each guest to choose a favourite. There was much turning of pages while this was going on and, under cover of the slight commotion, Bill whispered to me, 'I have bought a fine pair of mules.'

'Have you?' I replied, although I knew I was not supposed to talk. 'What have you called them?'

'Kindly Light and Loco Piff-Paff.'

Here Mr Hemans interrupted us with the number of a

133

hymn which he gave at random. I think he must have done this in order to stop us talking, for it turned out to be one that no one knew. The one after that, which was chosen by one of my partners at the Retreat dance, had seven verses and high bits in it but Bill was not disheartened for he soon began to talk again.

'I have found out that story about Rose Hall which you wished to hear about and I will tell it to you if you like.'

By four o'clock we were all very hot and my mother suggested that we should move up onto the verandah for tea, as it was cooler there. I do not think Beattie was sorry to get away from the piano and I was delighted at the thought of hearing the story Bill had promised to tell me.

After Bill had finished handing round cakes he sat down on a chair a little apart from the others and began his tale.

'Well, Bill, I don't like that story,' I said when he got to the end of the gruesome recital. 'Do you believe it can be true?'

'It is,' he replied. 'If another history of Jamaica were written that story would have to be put in it.'

At dinner, when all our friends had said goodbye and we were alone once more, I brought up the subject of the Rose Hall murder and asked my father if the tale were really a true one. He assured me that it was quite true and added that messengers bringing money from the bank at Falmouth were still unable to travel singly for fear of being attacked and murdered.

'Then do they go armed?' I asked, my eyes wide in astonishment.

'No,' he replied. 'Two or three people together will not be attacked for fear one should escape and act as a witness.'

Here my mother broke in to say she did not consider this

a fit subject for us to talk about and my father answered, 'She's not a child,' and there it ended.

But Bill's story haunted me for days and I tried, but failed, to find some likeness between the faithful servants who surrounded us and those who had murdered their employer at Rose Hall and drunk his brains mixed in rum as a talisman to prevent them from being discovered. Jack, our butler, had served our family faithfully all his life. Mary, the cook, had done the same. No one knew how old she was but she ruled the maids in the kitchen with determination and turned out our delicious meals on an open fire and a small charcoal burner.

Jack's matrimonial arrangements puzzled me. He possessed a daughter who was being brought up in the house and he was very fond of her. Before parties, father and daughter sat on a bench outside the downstairs pantry and together beat up innumerable eggs which were later turned into cakes. Miriam, the daughter, did not wear head kerchiefs like the other maids but had her black, woolly hair plaited into pigtails which stuck out all over her head. This form of hairdressing was, I gathered, a sign of independence and superiority and this superiority Miriam also showed in her manner to the other household servants. And yet ... and here came the puzzle ... Johanna, the head housemaid, was her mother.

After I had been in Jamaica a few months, I found that my mother was grieved that Jack refused to marry Johanna but she hoped that, for his daughter's sake, he would relent and do so. My father, on the other hand, discouraged any interference in his butler's private arrangements.

Every Sunday, Jack went to church on a mule in the pomp and glory of duck trousers, patent leather shoes, a black cutaway coat, a panama hat and with a big gold watch-chain looped across a brightly coloured waistcoat. Johanna, about the same time, disappeared to the village with her print petticoats girthed up into a roll round her waist and showing her bare feet and legs.

One morning, early, when I was returning from a run with Bundle, my dog, I found a little clay doll stuck onto a prong of the big front gate. I had already allowed the gate to swing to before I noticed it and the impact jerked it off or I might not have noticed that it had been placed there. When I stooped to examine it as it lay in the grass at my feet, I saw that it was a rough imitation of a human figure, about two inches in length, and that a pin had been stuck in its body. I examined this doll, picked it up, turned it over in my hand and then, with a feeling of distaste, put it back on the gate. It was too grotesque to be a child's plaything and, on close inspection, too dirty to be carried up to the house and exhibited as a curiosity. I whistled to Bundle and turned to run up the drive but he had taken advantage of my momentary inattention to be off on the trail of a mongoose. When, hot and exhausted, I had at last caught him in a bamboo thicket and scolded him for disobedience, all recollection of the little clay doll had gone from my mind. So, instead of rushing back full of my find as I might have done, I thought nothing more about it until we were all assembled at breakfast. Then my announcement caused a commotion. Albert dropped a dish, Jack hit him a resounding smack and they both retired out of the room, leaving us with nothing to eat.

My father looked serious. When the two servants returned to gather up the broken dish and to carry round the other dishes, he told Jack to send Peter, the gardener, down to the gate to bring up the clay figure but this proved impossible, the little doll having disappeared.

When breakfast was over, my father called me onto the front steps where no one could overhear us and asked if I had noticed anything peculiar about the doll.

I answered at once, 'Yes, it had a pin stuck in it.'

'Where?'

'In its side.'

He walked up and down for a minute or two in silence and, full of curiosity, I enquired, 'What was it?'

'Obeah,' he said. 'Someone has a grudge against a member of the household. We shall be lucky if there is not further trouble.'

All that day Jack crept about looking frightened. His normally glossy face was grey and leached and he looked as if he expected misfortune to fall on him.

The next morning the houseboy disappeared. He packed up his few possessions and walked out without asking permission or giving notice. Later the gardener came to say that he must go home to take medicine. He certainly did not look well, and was at once given leave of absence.

Then the trouble spread to the stables. The horses were not brought in from the pasture. My father was not able to drive to the office and the stable boys (with the exception of Peterkin who refused to be influenced by the general panic) shut themselves into their rooms. Finally Jack retired to bed with a severe pain in his side and the doctor was sent for.

His illness acted like a charm.

Peter returned looking sheepish but restored to normal health, the houseboy reappeared from no one knew where and took up his duties once more, the stable boys unbarred their bedroom doors and fetched the horses in from the pasture. Only Jack remained unchanged and, in spite of many visits from the doctor and of his reiterated pronouncements that his patient was suffering from no known illness, Jack nearly died.

Then, one morning, a good-looking young girl from the village arrived to ask my mother if she would give her a reference as housemaid to a family who lived near Kingston. From that moment, Jack began to recover. Soon he was able to sit in the sun and to reply to enquiries after his health, much as one who had been miraculously brought back from the gates of death.

There seemed to be no obvious connection between these events but, all the same, the servants seemed relieved and settled down again contentedly to their work.

Jack, however, still refused to marry Johanna and later took up with another good-looking girl in the village.

CHAPTER 16

The Valley, Rio Bueno

JACK WAS NO SOONER BETTER than my mother fell ill. She stayed in bed and there was much running to and fro with cans of hot water, freshly dried towels and jugs of cooling drinks; when I skipped into her big bedroom and looked at her sitting up in the middle of her four-poster bed, she told me that it was only an attack of malaria and that she would soon be up and about again.

However, the fever did not go as quickly as she had expected. One day the doctor drove up from Falmouth and the following day my father announced that he had advised a change to the hills for her. Like all changes in our household, this one had been arranged down to its minutest details before we heard of it. Beattie was to go with Mother to Mandeville and they were to stay there for three weeks or more until after the rainy season (which we were to expect at Arcadia at any moment) was over.

Mother and Beattie soon packed and departed in the big buggy for Mandeville and I was left alone with my father at Arcadia.

Almost at once the weather became unsettled; not a day passed without a downpour and the sun shone only at intervals. Then, for a short spell of about a fortnight, the weather improved. The heavy clouds passed inland, the sea breeze blew steadily once more and we had a succession of hot bright days.

My mother's illness and departure to Mandeville was

quickly followed by another and, for me, a more serious shock. My first intimation of this was the sound of my father's voice, 'Go on, take her carefully.'

I had been reading a copy of *Cornhill Magazine* in the Library and rushed out when I heard his words and the clatter of horse's hooves.

My father was standing, as was usual at that time of the morning, at the top of the front steps smoking a big cigar. An elderly Jamaican on a mule was sitting below him. Behind this stranger, dragging reluctantly on a rope, was my dear Victoria. And in the distance I could see Peterkin, my stable boy, holding a wild-eyed chestnut pony.

'Do as I tell you,' repeated my father. 'Take her slowly.' Then, turning to me, he said, 'Victoria is going back to the pen. That (with a wave of his hand to Peterkin and the chestnut) is your new mount.'

I suppose many girls would have been pleased enough to have any horse to ride and would have made no fuss had one been changed for another. However, loving Victoria as I did, I felt her departure and the arrival of the new pony bitterly.

As if he expected me to make some effort to prevent Victoria going, my father laid his hand heavily on my shoulder. But I stood perfectly still, glaring down the steps, loathing and hating everybody and everything above, below and around me – my eyes blinded with tears and my heart too proud to let me make a complaint. I had not received a word of warning to prepare me for this shock and I did not receive a word of sympathy now that the blow had fallen.

I fled with little more sound than a shadow makes when clouds are racing before the wind. I slipped from the portico and ran to the only place in the house where I could hope to find solitude, the lavatory. It was round a corner and down some steps. There I could cry until I was exhausted. Of course I loved Victoria.

However, I was wrong. Very soon I learnt to love Coquette (as the new little chestnut was called). She was wild and scary but that kept me wide awake and she could go like the wind. Later, when I taught her to jump and entered her in the riding competitions at local shows, she made a name for herself.

The first long ride I took on Coquette was not altogether a pleasant experience. When we had first gone out to Jamaica, it had been the custom for Jack to open the letter bag in the back hall at Arcadia. I could remember many days (especially those on which the mail from England arrived) when Beattie and I had waited impatiently while Jack sat balanced with the letter bag on a stool fumbling interminably with the lock. My outgoing correspondence consisted of a weekly letter to each of my brothers and an occasional scrawl to a girlfriend. The replies to those came at uncertain intervals. Sometimes I had written to Kingston for a roll of film for my Kodak and once I had sent for blue muslin to make into handkerchiefs.

All the ingoing and outgoing letters could have borne the scrutiny of the most critical parent but, all the same, when my father had returned from England, he had tightened many rules of the house. Amongst other things, he had given orders that the letter bag was to be opened on the verandah in his presence and that all outgoing main correspondence should be brought to him before being posted. One letter already, apart from our first one, had come from Mr Biggar and had been handed out by my father without comment. In it Mr Biggar had advised us to leave the theory alone until I was older and, in the meantime, to study individuals, in particular what he called the persistent personal tragedy to be found in most lives. I had followed his advice but, having up to that point only seen a sort of grotesque comedy lying hidden in all unsuccessful effort, I had hardly known where to begin. I could not find any 'sorrow patiently borne' which Mr Biggar expected me to describe. Still I had done my best and had, in fact, produced a group of sketches which were as melancholy as anyone could wish to read.

I had therefore written to Mr Biggar asking for advice and had worked and striven to do as he had advised me. The neat bundle I had to post contained the sketches and a short note which read as follows:

Dear Mr Biggar – Thank you for your criticism. I have tried to see the persistent personal tragedy in the lives of the people around me. It was not easy. Nothing much happens here.

Hoping you will like the stories and forgive me for bothering you.

Sincerely yours

Diana Lewes

In spite of the fact that there was nothing contraband in my notes or stories, I did not want to let my father read them. To give the parcel to Jack and to ask him to post it would have been clandestine and wrong, so the only thing left for me was to post the parcel myself.

Duncans, our nearest post office, was six miles away. It was a pleasant ride along the Upper Road down a valley to the sea but I did not want to say at dinner that I had been there for, Duncans obviously meant the post office.

The only other post office within reach was Clark's Town so, although it was further away than Duncans and although the weather looked unsettled, I made up my mind to ride there immediately after lunch.

Now if I had stopped to reflect, I should soon have realised that this expedition, like the one Alice Reay and I had made to Retreat, was destined to be unfortunate. But being young and enthusiastic, I was too eager to go to Clark's Town to notice that the omens were not entirely propitious.

When I asked Jack if one of the stable boys would be able to go with me that afternoon, he wriggled deprecatingly as he always did when forced to refuse a request.

'Him no can go, Young Misses,' he said sorrowfully. 'Devan, him lose him shoe dis marnin'; him go to de blacksmith dis arternoon. An' de udder mule hab got girth gall – berry bad – an' Massa say him no to go out till him well.'

So that was that! Both the stable mules being unavailable, I cast round in my mind for another companion. I should never have thought about an escort had Victoria still been with me but my new mount was so excitable that I fancied that she might go better in company.

'Doesn't the mutton woman go that way today?' I said at last.

'Yes, Misses.'

Here Jack was overcome by some unaccountable emotion which caused him to clasp his hands and turn from me. It was strange how mention of the mutton woman always called forth some display of feeling. What could it be about this woman that made her fellow servants act so strangely when she was mentioned?

'Well, Jack,' I said firmly, 'if she is going that way, surely I can go with her. She will be company on the road.'

Punctually at two o'clock, Coquette was brought round to the front door and I mounted and rode her to the servants' entrance. There stood a large mule saddled with panniers which were full to overflowing. Perched on those sat a plump black woman in a pink print dress, a bright bandana handkerchief on her head and a large jippa-jappa hat over all. Looking at her, it struck me that I had never seen anyone who looked less like a rider. Round her the house servants were assembled, but these scattered and fled as soon as they saw me, revealing the surprising fact that, in spite of being mounted, the mutton woman had left her reins trailing on the ground and that the mule was still fastened by a rope to an iron ring by the door.

Realising that, unless she dismounted or unless someone came to her aid she was likely to remain where she was, the little woman broke into a string of ejaculations which she addressed to the mule.

'Lard! What fo yo stan' dere! Can't yo see dat de Young Misses am ready?'

Her cries brought Jack, who had not, in my opinion, been far off. But his arrival only threw my riding companion into still greater confusion.

'Ignorant black woman,' he shouted, 'what fo yo keep Young Misses waiting? Doan I tell yo already long time dat Young Misses leave at two o'clock punctual time?'

'What fo you blaspheme me, Sah?' wailed the mutton woman. 'Doan I sit heah on de mule's back already fo half an hour?'

The reference to the mule drew Jack's attention to the fact that he was still tethered and, in another minute, he had called Albert and bidden him unfasten the head rope of the mule.

Then, with a heave and much creaking of the laden baskets, the big mule turned about and proceeded down the back drive.

Our journey thus commenced, the mutton woman and I made our way out of the back gate, across the common and presently found ourselves in Arcadia village. Here I discovered that Coquette and the mule did not make ideal travelling companions. They reminded me of the old ditty:

De harse an de mule were goin' out to pasture
Sing song sittie, won't yo ky me oh.
Said de harse to de mule, can't yo go a lickle faster.
Sing song sittie, won't yo ky me oh.

The mule had one pace – a run – and Coquette fretted whenever he came near her, laid back her ears and kept me in a continual state of anxiety lest she should gallop off. The mutton woman herself had exaggerated ideas of sociability. Every person we met on the road seemed to know her and, although she exerted enough self-control to remain silent until they had passed, she later shouted continuously to them until the last little group of people had dropped too far behind for their replies to be audible.

I bore this aggravating clamour till we reached the main road – my Roman Road! There, after a curt nod to my noisy companion, I set Coquette into a fast canter and was soon far away.

For a few minutes I could hear her peacock-like cries; then, all was peace and quiet. Coquette, when allowed to go at her own pace, was a perfect mover, her footfalls were muffled in the thick dust of the road, breaths of soft air fanned my cheeks and ears. I was perfectly happy.

For five, ten, twenty minutes we had continued in this manner and, by four o'clock, I had posted my letter and was on my way back. Thinking that I had made good time and that I should be home in time for a bath before dinner,

I pulled up at a spot where a country road branched off from the main road. Close at hand, guinea grass was thick in white dust; further back, low hills were covered to their crests in masses of green scrub; enormous cotton trees with roots like the buttresses of a cathedral stood on either side of the road. As I waited there I realised that the wind had dropped and that heavy clouds were stationary in the west. Everything was still.

Then, suddenly, a flock of birds came up from behind me and flew over my head. Even had they not screamed I should have known they were parrots by the quick beat of their wings. And for a second or two before they disappeared over the hills they showed up green against the black of the clouds.

I had been trying to make up my mind whether I should go home the way I had come or by the short cut through the hills. The parrots decided the matter for me. 'Go on,' I said to Coquette and we descended into the bush; further and further and deeper and deeper into the gloom we sank. Most heartily I soon longed for the bright open spaces by the sea, for the cane pieces and the plantations I knew so well. And then suddenly it began to rain.

To say it rains gives no idea of what really happens in the hills in Jamaica. There was nothing gentle or mild about that rain, nothing that could remind one even remotely of England. If Coquette and I had galloped under a waterfall, we could not have been more completely stunned, blinded and breathless. Gallantly the chestnut kept on and, because I could do no better, I gave her the length of the reins, hoping that with her eyes near the ground she would be able to see where we were going. Once or twice we brushed heavily against bushes. These seemed to be now on this side and now on that. Then suddenly they were everywhere. Long twigs clutched at my elbows and knees and the touch of them made me realise that somehow Coquette and I must have left the road.

My first action after coming to this conclusion was to take a pull at my horse's mouth. But, instead of coming to a halt, Coquette first increased her pace and then went rushing down a flat slide. She must have been on slippery rocks when I tried to stop her and this action must have upset her balance and precipitated the fall. A sheer cliff was now behind us and, before us, a path winding through thick bushes.

At this stage, the rain stopped as quickly as it had begun and, looking round me, I could see that my plight was an awkward one. I was wet and shivering with cold, I did not know where I was and, when I got off and tried to walk, I slipped and stumbled helplessly.

After progressing for a few yards in this way, I realised that I should be better off on Coquette's back than I was on my feet, so I mounted once more and she scrambled quickly to the bottom of the steep hill. The path showed no signs of petering out and my spirits began to rise. I now felt that I had embarked on an adventure and that, with every turn or twist in our road, a surprise might be waiting for me.

Coquette walked briskly on until we came to a second little pocket in the land. It was then that a loud squeal broke the silence. Some animal had come over the brow of the next hill and was advancing towards us. Coquette stopped at the first sound and, bracing herself, jumped, all four feet together, into the thick bush beside the path.

When I had freed my head and face from the branches among which we had landed, I looked up anxiously to see what was coming. The path, at this point, was more or less flat and straight and, along this open space, came a large black sow. She was squealing as only a pig squeals under the butcher's knife and she was running at top speed. All the Jamaican domestic pigs I had seen were black and lean and this one was like all the others. But, in the gloom, she looked blacker and leaner. Still a sow is nothing to be afraid of and I was just about to draw a breath of relief when I realised that the sow was not the only animal coming down the path.

Behind her came at least seven or eight little pigs, all running and squealing. And behind them came a big mule. It was this latter which made my heart stand still for he was evidently intent on catching and killing the big sow and all the little pigs. His head was down low on the ground, his mouth was open and his teeth were gleaming white and wicked and not more than a foot or two behind the last of the little pigs. It was only the roughness of the path and the pigs' agility which saved them, for he was galloping at a great pace.

This odd cavalcade passed without any of them noticing me or Coquette and soon the high squealing of the pigs and the clattering of the mule's hooves over-topped the next rise and ceased as suddenly as they had begun. Coquette stepped delicately out of the thick bushes and, apparently paying no further attention to the death struggle which might be going on in her animal world, walked briskly on. I had known her to shy from an old piece of machinery lying on the roadside but this exhibition of ferocity on the mule's part now left her perfectly calm. Her indifference lent me courage and the presence of the pigs indicated that there might be a house nearby where I could find someone to give us directions.

This surmise proved correct for the path soon showed signs of being more regularly used and a sudden turn brought us out onto a little clearing and disclosed just what I had been hoping to see – a hut. The sound of rushing water had been growing louder and here it filled the open space. Over a rocky bed ran a torrent which cut the clearing in two and completely barred our way. On the far side stood a native hut made of palm branches. But it was neither the torrent nor the hut which surprised me and pulled me up sharp; I had expected to see the torrent and the hut. It was the two humans standing above the water on the far bank who took me completely by surprise. There were two men, one big and the other small, on the point of fighting. The bigger one of the two was, I felt sure, animal-suave in character; the smaller one simple-pleasing or perhaps pleasing. The bigger of the two was dark and powerfully built; the smaller fair and thin and they were both white. I was surprised to see the two of them in such squalid surroundings.

Like Englishmen who are about to fight, they had nothing in their hands and were relying on their fists to inflict as much damage as possible. And they were both too engrossed in their occupation to notice me. The animal-suave man stooped over the little one threatening him with his big clenched fists and, through all the rush of the water, I could imagine the insults he must be hurling at his opponent. The little man, not at all daunted, drew back his skinny arm and I waited to see his clenched fist shoot up to the ugly face of the other.

Then, before anything could happen, before the smaller man could hit the bigger man or the latter kill the former, a high thin squealing came, once more, from over the hill. Coquette heard it and raised her head. The two men heard it and, looking in the direction of the sound, saw me.

I have never seen two people look so surprised. They

did not drop their clenched fists but stood there, by the riverside, staring at me and looking helpless and a little ridiculous.

Meanwhile I thought, 'The sow is coming back and so is the mule and the little pigs too or as many of them as have survived,' and, thinking this, I forgot the two men and concentrated my attention on the bush and on what might come out of it.

The noise of squealing quickly grew louder. It even out-did the noise of the rushing water. The certainty that they would shortly be disturbed drove the men to take action. They both dropped their threatening attitudes and came slowly forward. The little man looked anxiously at me, the big man was watching the path and, when the sow came rushing out, he crossed the river with great agility. I believe he and the pigs came past each other on the rocks in midstream. But it was the mule he was after for, jumping in its way, he threw up his long arms to their full extent, thus forcing it to remain on my side of the water. It was evident that he wished to separate the pigs and mule but I was not comfortable at being forced to remain so close to that diabolic creature. However, he shouted for a halter and, having caught it when it was thrown to him, quickly secured the mule, led it to the other side of the river and tied it to a tree.

Meanwhile the sow and piglets had run straight into the hut and there had ceased their clamour but not their power to disturb for, out of the dilapidated dwelling, arose the cry of a child.

The small man abandoned his scrutiny of Coquette and me and turned reluctantly to offer some help but, before he was able to do anything, a young woman with a child in her arms came out of the hut. She was thin and pale, as white women are when forced to do hard work in a tropical climate. She looked ill, as did the baby in her arms, and I wondered how these three people had come to be in such a strange place and how long they would be able to remain alive in such surroundings.

As to myself, peace having been restored by the return of the sow and the piglets into an enclosure at the back, I began to realise that I was cold and that my clothes were soaked. Seeing that the three inhabitants of the lonely valley did not intend to come to my help, I became impatient. Being sure that my voice could not carry across the river, I resorted to a dumb show. Pointing in the direction of the path by which I had come, I moved my hand rapidly to and fro with the fingers extended trying at the same time to throw into my attitude all the loathing and dislike I felt for that, the only exit I knew. Then, looking round at the three who had assembled on the further bank, I swept my arm around in a circular movement, mutely begging them to tell me if there was another way out.

They all understood what I meant. The woman at once began to urge the men to go to my help but, to my surprise, instead of doing so, they recommenced their quarrel.

The big man stepped up to the small man and shook his clenched fist in his face. It seemed that I was, after all, going to be a witness of the fight. However, the woman intervened and, with a gesture which betrayed a mixture of despair and exasperation, she stepped between them, her back to the simple-pleasing and facing the animal-suave and, holding the still-crying baby against her shoulder, she said something which decided the matter. For, with a last furious gesture, the animal-suave turned and walked down the clearing.

The two who were left standing before the hut watched

until he had gone a little distance, as if to assure themselves that he was not likely to change his mind and that he really did intend to lead me out of the valley, and then signed to me to follow. Nodding my thanks, I engineered Coquette across the river, past the tethered mule and quickly followed my guide. He had made his way to the end of the clearing and then plunged into another track which did not lead up over the hills but bent down to the low lands which had been cleared here and there for the cultivation of yams, cho-chos and other vegetables and, eventually, made its way to the foot of the ridge along which the road to Arcadia passed.

Once having recognised the general lie of the land, I felt more comfortable in my mind and was able to follow my guide without any misgivings. He strode along glancing neither to the right nor to the left and never once looking round to see if Coquette and I were following him, quite evidently engrossed in his own furious reflections and anxious only to have done with us and to be free to return to the interrupted quarrel. Riding quietly in this way, I began to think that, in this sparsely populated island, it seemed possible to meet with the greatest extremes in riches and poverty, good and evil and love and hate. There was, as far as I could see, nothing trivial in this tropical life and nothing detached. Only Beattie and I seemed to stand alone. We were like visitors from an entirely different existence.

Then I went on to think of the three people I had seen that afternoon. They were all poorly clad. In fact, the two men were more or less in rags. I wondered how they had got into the state which they were in and how long they had been living in that forsaken spot. Curious as I was, I did not feel anxious to put any questions to the man striding in front of me. He did not look as if he would welcome conversation.

One last steep climb took us up to the road and there, without even a gesture of farewell, he left. One second he was standing on the open road, the light of the sinking sun reflected on his damp face and on the muscles of his arms and shoulders, the next he was plunging down into the valley again.

Coquette and I took very little time to reach home. Fortunately no one had noticed my absence; my father was not even aware that I had been out. Only Jack was hanging about the back door when I cantered up, but that was probably because he hoped to hear how I had got on with the mutton woman. However, I did not satisfy his curiosity. So much had happened since I had started on my ride that the mutton woman already seemed remote. One thing I did ask Jack as I kicked my foot out of the stirrup and slid down onto the ground: 'Do you know who those white people are who live down in the Rio Bueno valley?'

At my words the look of expectancy left his face and was succeeded by a blank stare.

'Me no know, Misses,' he replied.

This, the regular Jamaican denial, might mean 'I don't know', 'I do not want to know', or 'I don't want Young Misses to know'. However, I knew I was up against a blank wall and that I would find out nothing from him.

Those people haunted me for days. I did not like to ask my father about them as it was difficult for me to explain how I came to meet them. It was, I knew, no good asking Jack again. No one could be more obtuse than he if he wanted to be. Henry, whom I questioned on the way to church, evidently knew nothing of them. I really believe that in order to please me he would have made up some story and I begged him not to trouble. Peterkin, the last I questioned, frankly replied that he did not know anything of the white people living in that valley but, if the Young Misses wished, he would find out. He had relations living at Clark's Town and could go round that way next time he went to visit them.

By the time Peterkin's half-day arrived, I had a parcel of a tin of infant food, sweets and biscuits made up for the baby and this I entrusted to him. Although I waited late that night, he did not come to the house with a message and it was not until the following afternoon that I met him by chance coming across the pasture with a basket of naseberries.

'Did you take that parcel?' I asked crossly.

'Yes, Misses.'

'Then why didn't you come up and tell me last night – were you too late?'

'No, Misses, not late.'

'Then why?' I persisted.

'Me did come up, Young Misses, but Jack no let me see Young Misses. Missie gone to bed.'

'What time was that?' I asked.

'Eight.'

'But that was ridiculous,' I exploded, 'I don't go to bed at eight o'clock.'

'Me know berry well Young Misses no go to bed at eight o'clock. But it better for me no to say so. Mr Jack no want Young Misses for to know 'bout de Buckra family in de Rio Bueno valley.'

'Peterkin,' I said, 'who are those people?'

'Me no know how dem name, Young Misses, but me think dem come from Dry Bottom in Saint James.'

This name meant nothing to me but I believed that, if Peterkin really did not know any more than this, I must be satisfied with this information as being sufficient.

CHAPTER 17

Oxford (3)

ABOUT THIS TIME I noticed that Herr Bauer was coming more frequently to Arcadia. I do not mean to say that he either lunched or dined often with my father and me or even that he occasionally dropped in for tea. He did none of these things. His calls were not what one might have described as social ones. He never turned up when one might reasonably have expected him and, among other things, he cleverly avoided me. And yet, on looking back over a fortnight or so, I realised that he had come very often. Sometimes he arrived just before my father set out for the office, making some excuse that he was on his way to a distant property and that he wished to make sure that his employer knew of his whereabouts. Sometimes he drove up after lunch when we were on the verandah and disturbed my father's rest and smoke. From my post of vantage above the portico, I could hear his harsh voice droning on and on but never the gist of his conversation. Sometimes he came after tea when I was out riding and, once or twice, I saw his buggy drawn up by the front door early in the morning before my father was dressed for the day.

When I watched my father smoking his big cigars and walking to and fro on the front portico, he seemed to me to be a strong man in a difficult position. I noticed that after Mother and Beattie left he began to complain of my brother's school expenses, of the rates and taxes he had to pay on his big house in England which he had not been able to sell and even, sometimes, of the weekly expenses at Arcadia. This, from a man like him, meant a lot. He was, as a rule, easy-going and pleasure-loving and, although his personal expenses were small, he loved display and disliked economies. These complaints were always more bitter after one of the attorney's visits and this gave me the idea that they must be connected with those visits. Herr Bauer must, I thought, be putting pressure on my father, making use of the general disturbance in trade for his own ends. And again and again I asked myself, 'Why is this happening? Why is Herr Bauer doing this?'

One evening, after I had gone to bed, I heard a buggy drive up to the front and stop there. Reaching out, I pulled aside the mosquito net, seized the matches and lit a candle. Who could this possibly be but Herr Bauer? In no time, I was out on the verandah and running on bare feet to the north side of the house where, by leaning far out over the railing, I had a view of the portico.

It was a lovely night, with the scent of stephanotis blossoms, and of the tea roses and lilies growing in the garden below, heavy in the air. Candles were shining steadily in the portico and I could hear the clink of glasses and the drone of men's voices. Yes, I had been right, that was Herr Bauer's rough, unpleasant intonation and that, after a moment's interval, my father's more mellow tones.

On silent feet, I fled back to my room. From the wardrobe, I pulled out a new green muslin frock. Dancing slippers were the first that came to hand and black silk stockings. In no time I had dragged a comb through my hair and gathered my curls together with a red ribbon.

What my father thought when I arrived downstairs a few minutes later I do not know. I was too busy playing my part of hostess to notice and too determined to out-sit Herr Bauer to pay any attention to his ejaculations of surprise.

'No, I am not at all sleepy, thank you. How wise Herr Bauer is to make the most of this lovely night!'

Sooner than I could possibly have hoped, my most disconcerted guest rose to leave. But no sooner had he mounted into his buggy and whipped up his horses than I turned and fled through the house for, in spite of the success of my ruse, I did not feel equal to facing my father's interrogations. Besides I had learnt something during the short time I had sat chatting there which sent me to bed full of horror for, in those few minutes, Herr Bauer had mentioned Dry Bottom in Saint James. I realised that he must have been the man who had sold out those people I had met in the Rio Bueno valley.

My father made no reference to Herr Bauer's visit or to my unexpected incursion onto the portico when we met at breakfast the next morning. Perhaps his reserve was not surprising because the rains, which we had been waiting for, began that day in earnest.

Spring rains in that part of Jamaica begin early in May and last for three weeks. I woke to the roar of water on the shingle roof and listened all day to the gurgle of overburdened pipes and gutters. It was impossible for either my father or me to get out during those weeks and, after the first novelty of the situation had passed, I felt so depressed and ill that I had difficulty in preventing myself from bursting into tears for no reason whatsoever.

Shoes became mouldy and leather-bound books sprouted a thin coat of mildew. A sort of grey curtain shut in the house on every side. Every effort bathed me in perspiration. It was impossible to concentrate on any work. Still, idle as

I was and hot as the weather was, I shivered in the close damp air.

On my father, however, those three weeks of almost continuous rain had an exhilarating effect. From the verandah he supervised the gardener in his efforts to clear the gutters and drains, examined the house and outbuildings for leaks and overflows and noted down the daily fall when Jack came in, half soaked, with the brimming gauge.

In the newspapers, falls of eleven inches in the twenty-four hours were recorded and thrilling stories of rivers which had come down in flood filled the news columns. In one place, I read that a party of country women returning from market had been surprised. The road which they had to follow crossed a riverbed where it divided into two streams leaving a stony island in the middle. The women had negotiated the first of these shallow streams before they noticed that the water in the second branch of the river had turned a muddy colour. Filled with anxiety, for they knew by this that heavy rain must have fallen in the hills and that the river was about to come down in spate, they immediately turned and attempted to recross the portion which they and their donkeys had scrambled over a minute or two before. But it was too late. The river came down in a roaring flood and carried them all out to sea. In another place, women washing clothes in a rocky gully noticed that the water was changing colour and, at once, leaving their washing, they rushed up the bank to safety. One, however, stopped to gather up her bundle of clothes and was carried away and drowned. The only moments of relief during these days, apart from reading these stories in the newspapers, were the arrival of the post boy with the letter bag or the mutton woman with the joints and presents of fruit from the hill estates. All else was dull and uniformly drab.

I shall never forget the day the rain ceased and the sun came out once more. That morning my father called me up to the verandah and together we stood looking down onto the sea of cloud which obliterated the low land between us and the sea. Presently this white blanket was severed from top to bottom and the most wonderful view was disclosed. Each hill and valley, each cane field and even the coconut palms and trees one thousand feet below us were clearly visible and ninety or a hundred miles away the blue mountains of Cuba broke out on the horizon.

I was filled with delight. I felt proud that my father had known that this was about to happen.

Not only did the surrounding land spring into life, but immediately innumerable birds flew from tree to tree, pea-fowl and turkeys came trooping round the house and even the domestic poultry and the Muscovy ducks joined in the general rejoicing. That was a busy day for the household. Bedding was carried out and aired. Shoes and books were placed in rows in the sun and finally furniture and floors were re-polished. It seemed that the rains had gone as quickly and as completely as they had come and that we might now look forward to the usual hot weather. My father's remark of 'good pond rains' seemed a manly view to take of the past weather conditions and a fitting epitaph to a necessary period of discomfort.

A few days later my father suggested I should go to Philip for a change. I suppose I still looked washed out and I know I felt limp and tired so, in spite of my protests, it was arranged that I should go and thus began my third visit to Oxford.

I drove over one morning in a little two-wheeled trap,

which had been bought for me shortly before. As soon as I got to Oxford, Philip suggested we should put his pony (which he said would go in single harness) into my trap and go down to Falmouth to do the shopping. This seemed a good idea but, unfortunately, the pony did not live up to my brother's expectations. He bolted down the steep hill from the Busha House to the yard as soon as his head was let loose. I remember little of the accident which followed, except that Philip fell on top of me when we were thrown out of the trap and that he, afterwards, said I was harder than the stones in the yard, which was unkind considering he had hit me first.

Of course the next day I was terribly stiff, too stiff to go round the estate with Philip on horseback and I had to rest in the house instead of amusing myself as I had done on my last visit. Philip, still complaining of the hardness of my bones, went out about his business and I was left to a long day alone. However, I was really glad to stay quiet, as my side, where something sharp (probably a part of the buggy which had been smashed) must have dug into me, was very painful and I could not breathe without discomfort.

Dorcas, the black housekeeper, came in several times during the afternoon, once to tell me that the bookkeeper, who had witnessed the accident, had called to ask how I was and at about five she came in again to announce that a Mr Harrison, a neighbour, had called. I sent polite answers to these two messages but did not feel it necessary to see either of the men. When Philip came home I told him who had called and he said, 'Did you ask Harrison in?'

'No.'

'Then why not?'

'I did not feel like seeing him or anyone,' I explained.

'Well, you ought to have.'

'But Philip,' I expostulated.

'It's no good, he's a neighbour and you should have given him tea.'

There the conversation ended but I thought that, had Beattie been with me, she would have known what to do and would have prevented me from making this social blunder. I felt that one reproof from a member of my own generation was more galling and more difficult to bear than any amount of fault-finding by a parent.

Later Philip softened his reproof by presenting me with a long strip of sticking plaster which he said he had procured from the doctor in Falmouth and which I was to fasten tightly round above my waist, over the bruised ribs.

The next day I was, if anything, stiffer than ever. In spite of the supporting plaster, I could neither walk nor ride and had to reconcile myself to a second quiet day. Again, at about five o'clock, Dorcas came in to say that someone had called. This time it was Mr Ambrose.

Here, I thought, is an opportunity to show Philip I have taken his reproof to heart! 'Show him in please, Dorcas,' I said, struggling into a sitting posture.

A tall, thin man in a navy blue suit with a big bunch of violets in his button hole was shown in. I shook hands with him, explained my brother's absence and did my best to carry on what I hoped was a polite and suitable conversation. At first, he was shy and rather silent but, when I asked Dorcas to bring in tea, he unbent.

I asked him if he liked Jamaica. He said, 'I have never been anywhere else.'

'Then you must like it,' I replied cheerfully, 'for it is against nature not to like some place.'

After a pause, he added that he had always had a great wish to visit America.

'You will be disappointed with the voyage there,' I answered. 'I've heard the boats are small and the passengers odd. They spend all day asking each other to play cards.' As this evoked no reply, I presently asked him if he had any pets and, as an afterthought, any brothers and sisters.

His answer of, 'Yes, two,' left me in doubt as to whether he meant brothers, sisters or pets, so, hoping to clear the matter up, I said, 'Have you a bedroom to yourself or do you share with the others?'

'They are pigs,' he replied. 'I thought you said pets.'

When I had recovered from this shock, I asked him if he was interested in reading, if he could tell me anything about the Arawaks, if he knew the exact spot on the Drax Hall River where Columbus had landed and several other questions which I felt sure any really grown-up person should have been interested in. They each evoked the one answer, 'No.' I wished sincerely that Bill had been there with his list of suitable remarks but I did not like to get up and hunt for the morning's paper. To read a paragraph would, I felt, have been an admission of social failure.

At last, in despair, I admired his bunch of violets and asked how he had managed to grow them in such a hot climate. He, at once, took the flowers out of his button hole and offered them to me. I thought his visit was never going to end but, even though I was tired before he left, I was encouraged by the certainty that, in entertaining him, I was doing the right thing. I greeted Philip triumphantly when he walked in just before supper.

'You asked that man in?' Philip ejaculated in horror.

'Yes, wasn't that right?'

'Of course not. We never entertain him or his people. And he probably only called to ask me about some stock.'

My misfortunes did not end here. The next morning, and the next, a runner arrived with a bunch of freshly picked violets, and when I, too proud to hide them from my brother, placed them in vases about the room, he remarked disgustedly, 'There! I told you so!' Though what he had told me had not, as far as I could remember, included any reference to flowers.

A few days later, just after the post boy had arrived with the letters and welcome news from Mandeville, Philip told me that Father wished to see him on business and that he would have to go over to Arcadia. 'I can't take you with me,' he said, 'because, I expect the runners with the estates money tomorrow.'

I was eating my breakfast at the time and went on munching. 'Well,' I said between two mouthfuls of yam and rissole, 'I'll stay and look after the money if you like but what do I do with it?'

'You take the bag with the money and keep it here for one night,' he explained. 'The next day two more runners will come and you will open the bag – Alert, A–L–E–R–T is the letter lock – and hand out the two packets to them.'

'Do I keep the money here, in the house, for a night?'

'Yes.'

'Where?'

'Anywhere – anywhere you think safe.'

'Oh.'

One other thing Philip asked me before he drove away, and that was, 'Do you mind if I take my coachman with me? I shall want him at Arcadia to look after the horses?'

It did not seem to me that it made much difference if I minded being left without him or not. I was supposed to say, 'Oh, I don't mind,' and so I said it.

The first day and night after his departure passed

quietly. I rode round the estate and went to bed early. The next morning, at about eleven, Dorcas came to say that Willie, the runner, was on the back steps and that he wished to speak to me. I went out feeling rather important. Willie was a very tall Jamaican with white hair. He handed me a leather bag which I knew contained the money; it was heavy and fastened by a brass letter padlock. Down in the back yard I could see two other messengers with their mules and bags who were, I guessed, going on to the office.

'Thank you, Willie,' I said, taking the bag from him.

'Yes, Young Misses,' replied Willie, giving me a broad grin.

'Is that all?' I added presently.

'Yes, Misses.'

He did not, however, move.

'What is it, Willie?' I asked.

'Nuttin, Misses.'

Standing there, on the top of the steps, he was, to me, the picture of indecision. With one bare foot he began to caress the calf and shin of his other leg like an ungainly heron on a river's brink. Having accomplished this manoeuvre to his satisfaction, he put his first leg down and drew the other foot carefully up to the knee, leaving his big toe in front of the tibia and the little toes to the back. I was fascinated by this and even more interested in the expression on Willie's face. If he wished to say something before going away, I did not understand why he did not speak out. 'What is the matter?' I said at last. But my direct question was evidently not what he had been hoping for. As far as he and I were concerned, it did not unlock the riddle of his silence for, with a gusty sigh, he answered: 'No Misses, yes Misses, marnin' Misses' and, at that, ran quickly down to the bottom of the steps where he presently mounted and rode away with his companions.

This conversation and Willie's odd behaviour left me with a feeling of doubt in my mind. And, pondering what it could have meant, I put on my hat and walked down the hill into the yard. This I did partly with the intention of exercising my brother's two dogs and partly to see how the pic'ny gang was getting on in Philip's absence. The head of the gang was a jolly old Jamaican woman who was always dressed in so many petticoats and jackets that she gave the impression of being extremely stout. This may have been the case but I doubted it because her arms and legs were so thin. On her head she wore a large straw sun hat tied closely under her chin by a red bandana kerchief. To carry on a conversation with her, one had to stand directly in front and in line with her vision. I always wondered how, from the depths of her bonnet, she was able to keep such a vigilant watch on the mischievous black children who formed her gang.

She and I were good friends and I never passed through the yard without having a chat with her and enquiring after her husband whom she called 'Uncle Johnnie'.

On this particular morning, she was on the watch for me and hurried up, her petticoats swinging and her sun hat bobbing in the breeze. 'Marnin', me darlin' Young Misses,' she ejaculated. 'Me berry glad to see Young Misses.'

'And I am glad to see you too, Matilda,' I replied. 'How are the piccaninnies behaving this morning?'

'Berry or'nary, Young Misses. Dem children am mos' stro'nary tiresome. But Matilda am partic'lar pleased to see Young Misses.' Here the sun bonnet swept round in order that its owner might take a look at her tiresome

charges and I lost sight of her face and also the sound of
her voice. When both of these were returned to me, I was
startled by the vehemence of her words and the earnestness
of her expression. 'Me an' Uncle Johnnie will be praying
for yo tonight,' she concluded emphatically.

'It is nice of you, and of Uncle Johnnie too, to pray for
me,' I said slowly, 'but why tonight?'

'Doan we know dat you'll be alone in de house wid all dat
money!' cried Matilda.

'Does everyone know this?'

'O' course! Doan I say dat me an Uncle Johnnie will be
prayin' for yo!'

And so the secret was out. All the estates workers would
know that I had been left in charge at Oxford Busha House
and that the coachman had gone with Philip to Arcadia.

This immediately made me think of the bag, which I
had placed in my brother's desk which had no lock. So,
thanking Matilda, I said 'Goodbye,' whistled to the dogs
and walked back to the house. There I took the bag out of
the desk and, wrapping it up in my mosquito net, hid it
behind my bed.

After that, I hung about the house wondering if I was
not being unnecessarily disturbed by what Matilda had
said. By supper time, I had made up my mind that no
amount of hints were going to frighten me and that no
suggestions from the household servants would make me
alter my brother's rules and regulations in the smallest
way. Therefore, when Dorcas came at ten o'clock to ask me
if I would like her to sleep in the house with me, I said
crossly, 'No, certainly not.'

She must have seen by my manner that I was not to be
moved for she made no further effort to persuade me to let
her stay. Perhaps, at the same time, she was glad not to

have to sleep in the house and had only offered to do so because she thought she was bound to try and protect me. Her only request was that I should, before locking her out, go round the house and satisfy both her and myself that it was securely barred for the night.

After she had left and the back door had been locked, I stood listening to her retreating footsteps. They grew rapidly less and less distinct until, after a minute or two, I could hear them no more. Then I looked round the dark house feeling alone and cut off from the world. I did not, even yet, admit to myself that there was any likelihood of danger for me but, all the same, the position required consideration. I was alone but I had two small dogs with me, my brother's terriers, and with dogs I always felt safe and secure. Calling them to me, I picked up the candle and walked once more round the house, going into every room and opening every door. One after another they swung to behind me, so I collected books from the drawing room and propped them all open, my bedroom door included and, having assured myself that they could not now under any circumstances shut to during the night, I undressed and climbed into bed. In no time I was sound asleep, satisfied that the money in the leather bag was safely tucked away behind the mosquito curtains and that it was as secure as I could make it.

Some time during the night I was awakened by the dogs. It was dark and they were rushing together into the dining room, growling and snarling. I jumped out of bed and met the dogs coming back into my room. To my surprise, they went past me and between my feet and hurled themselves under the bed.

In the dining room, I hesitated, not knowing from which side of the house sounds had come to frighten the dogs before I woke and from which side danger threatened. And, while I stood there, the two animals crawled out from under the bed and rushed snapping and snarling to the back door.

I do not think that from the first I had any doubt that those people outside the back door had come to take the money and that to do so they would not hesitate to kill me. But, at the same time, I knew that they would reckon on surprise to assist them and on being able to break into the house before I woke.

Standing there, I knew that no one from the outside world would make any attempt to rescue me even if they should be aroused by an unexpected sound. Consequently it was no use screaming. If I were to save myself, I must keep a steady mind and stop my heart from jumping so desperately. 'Hush,' I whispered to the dogs and, in the stillness which followed, I listened and tried to think. We were standing about three feet or so from the back door. Almost, I could put out my hand and touch it. From the other side came a low sound of many voices hushed to a confused murmur. As I stared, fascinated, the door gave to invisible hands pressed against it and, when released, rattled against the bolt.

It was then that I remembered I had heard Philip say that there was a gun in the house. We had been talking about the ring-tail pigeon and he had said that he sometimes went shooting in the hills with friends. I tried hard to overcome my inertia and assert a clear picture upon the nothingness of my mind and, in the hope of getting some clue to the whereabouts of the gun, I turned hastily towards the drawing room. But it was no use. The moment I turned my back on the door, behind which I knew all those people were assembled, a panic filled my mind. I recalled the story of Rose Hall and how the murderers had drunk their employer's brains mixed in rum and my thoughts seemed to whirl around this one event, drawing closer and closer to it.

It was when I seemed to be approaching the centre of this whirl that I became aware of the situation as it would appear if I were standing twenty feet above the house: at the centre, a girl standing alone in the dark house, those people at the back door whispering and, all around the land. It was this picture in which I saw myself and my potential murderers that seemed to clear my mind and to restore my thoughts more to their correct sequence.

As soon as this had happened and I had reached a state of sufficient mental quiet, ideas began to crowd into my mind. I had no gun but I did not feel helpless. Reaching out behind me, I lifted one of the dining room chairs and, drawing it noiselessly to me, I clasped it to my chest. Then holding it in my arms, I spoke loudly and clearly.

'I know you are there!' I said. 'But what do you think this is?'

In the silence which followed my words I allowed the heavy chair to drop on to one leg and there I held it balanced.

'It's a gun,' I went on, 'and, if you don't go before I count ten, I will fire through the panels of the door.'

The dogs, which had been crowding round my bare feet, sprang away at the fall of the chair but I had no time to spare for them. Taking a deep breath, I began to count slowly and steadily.

'Four ... Five ... Six ... '

Was that a sound outside? I dared not stop to listen ...

'Seven ... Eight ... '

What in the world should I do if I reached the end of

my count and the men had not gone? Should I go on indefinitely or should I stop? And my voice was trembling. It must not.

'Nine ... Ten.'

That last word, at any rate, rang out clearly without the suspicion of a tremor.

My bare feet were dimly reflected in the polished boards of the floor. The dogs came creeping back till I could feel their hairy bodies pressed against me. The contact of something living was comforting. When I was able to think, I realised that, except for them, I was alone.

I put the chair back in its place, hugged the dogs in turn and walked soberly back to my room.

Next morning, I was wakened from a sound sleep. It was seven o'clock. Dorcas was tapping on the back door. Before I let her in, I gathered up the books and put them away in the drawing room. They, more than the chair, had saved my life for, had anyone got into the house before I had woken, nothing would have saved me.

Dorcas went about her work as if nothing had happened, as if, had things fallen out differently, she might not have been called on to view something different. When the runners arrived, I went to my bedroom, pulled out the money bag from behind my bed, opened it, took out the two packets, returned to the door and thrust these at them without saying a word. 'They knew,' I thought.

In the yard, none of the workers spoke to me. They seemed to avoid my glances until Matilda came up and, placing herself immediately in front of me, said: 'Doan I tell Young Misses dat me an' Uncle Johnnie would be prayin' for yo?' There was reproach in her voice and she confronted my hot, angry face with kindliness. A picture of two white-haired Jamaicans kneeling, praying to God through the night for a child of an alien race sprang into my mind.

'Thank you Matilda, and please thank Uncle Johnnie too,' I said penitently.

Later, when Philip returned from Arcadia with the coachman and the horses, he found the whole estate depressed but, whether that was because they had failed to kill me or whether it was because they were ashamed to think how near they had come to doing so, I could not make out. Anyhow he was not able to help me out of this difficulty because I never told him anything of what had happened.

CHAPTER 18

The Promises

WHEN I GOT HOME I found that my mother and Beattie had returned from Mandeville. Mother was quite strong again and Beattie looked positively pink-cheeked.

Mother's fresh energy showed itself at once. As soon as she and Beattie had got over their long drive home, she announced that it was time to send out invitations for the 'Busha' party which was an annual institution. To this party all the Bushas, the office staff and some of the bookkeepers were invited. Therefore, immediately after lunch on the day after their return, Beattie sat down to copy out invitations and I addressed envelopes and it was not until it was too late to go out for either a walk or a drive that we were released from this occupation.

Evenings at Arcadia were boring. My father was fond of a game of whist and, being just four in number, there was no escape for us girls. Night after night, a serge tablecloth was spread over one of the iron tables on the verandah, the silver candlesticks were carried up by Jack and we settled down to what Beattie and I looked on as our special purgatory.

This routine of the tablecloth, the candlesticks and the cards was interrupted only on Sundays when we were allowed to read and on occasional party evenings when my father's friends came to play poker.

As far as entertainment was concerned, dinner was not

172

much more lively than whist. Mother and Beattie carried
on most of the conversation that night. My father ate in
silence and I fell into my usual habit of dreaming dreams
and imagining what I would do in the most impossible
situations. In the dining room something I had never seen
lived invisibly. When Jack and Albert had cleared the table
and carried the trays of plates and glasses through the
back hall and out into the night, this something that lived
in the room would creep out and wrap itself round me.
From where I sat at table I might, with my eyes, watch
Albert disappear with his load bound for the scullery but
all the time I was really only conscious of this invisible
something which waited for this moment to make itself
felt. It was a presence which made me happy. The grown-
ups might talk as they would but, once this living,
breathing something came out of the corners of the room
where it had fled during the bustle of the meal, I was safe
and nothing could hurt me.

On this evening I had drifted a long way.

When Mother rose, I returned so suddenly and got up in
such a hurry that I nearly fell and sent my chair sliding
over the polished floor. My father did not move and, at
first, I think it was my clumsiness that made him hold out
his hand to bid me stay. But it was not this that was on his
mind. 'Sit down,' he said, motioning to me to retrieve my
chair. 'I want to speak to you.'

Mother looked at him and then at me. And I thought she
must be anxious for she hesitated in the doorway while
Beattie walked steadily on up the stairs. As far as I can
remember, she said, 'Leave the child alone, Harry.' But I
cannot be sure because there were times when my father
made me feel frightened and I did not know if this was
going to be one of them. When she had gone and he and I

were alone, I pulled my chair close to the table and sat down with my hands folded in front of me. What was my father going to say to me, I wondered, and why had he chosen this time and allowed my mother and sister to go up to the verandah without me?

In the silence which followed I prayed earnestly that he would not ask me anything that I might find difficult to answer. When, however, he began to speak, I realised at once that no amount of thought could have prepared me for what he was about to say.

'Do you ever think of getting married?' he asked quietly, 'because I should advise you not to. If ever you do so, you go out of my house and I shall never speak to you again.'

So marriage was to be the subject of our conversation. I was so surprised that I had nothing to say and he continued uninterrupted. 'I suppose you know what happened to your half-brother John?' Yes, I knew what had happened to my half-brother. He had been ten years older than me and, when I was a little girl, had married someone my father did not approve of and we had never seen him again. My father's threat, therefore, was not what people would call 'an idle one'. Although how any threat which frightened people and forced them into telling lies could be idle, I did not know.

'Well,' he said, prompting me to speak.

'No,' I replied as steadily as I could. 'I have never thought of getting married.' Then I suddenly remembered Mr Cameron and wondered if, by any chance, Mother had told him of my proposal. But, on second thoughts, this did not seem likely. Besides I did not love Mr Cameron and had never thought of marrying him.

'That is just as well,' my father went on. 'You know now what would happen to you if you did.'

All this time a sort of terrible nervousness had been mounting steadily inside me. It burnt the back of my eyes, gripped my throat and made my inside tremble so much that I was afraid that I might be sick. I suppose nearly every girl is interested in someone. It was the fear that my father might, before he had done, hit upon the one man whom I liked but had not yet dared to think of in this light that made me feel so nervous. He, however, began with my English friends and went through them one at a time finding in each one some defect which made him unsuitable for matrimony or some disadvantage which was, in his eyes, insurmountable and, at the end of each little personal history, my father looked up at me quickly and said, 'Promise me you will not marry him.' And each time I promised.

After a time we got to my Jamaican friends.

Poor Bill came first; his only fault was that he was hard up and had a mother and sister to support. Although I did not love Bill, I was ashamed of the relief I felt when he was mentioned and of the celerity with which I replied, 'Yes, I promise.' Bill was so good and kind that he deserved to have someone who would answer bravely for him.

The next on the list was a man who sometimes came to play tennis with us and whom I had once partnered in a small tournament. He was too old. Had I not, my father said, noticed that he wore a wig? My goodness, a wig! Did lack of hair prevent a man from being a good husband? Still, at sixteen, wigs, false teeth or trusses were not attractive and it was with a sigh of relief that I again agreed. The polo players came next: they were a wild lot. Then there were the men who came to sing hymns on Sundays and my partners at the Retreat dance. I did not know how he had heard of them all, or how he could remember all their names. But not one was left out.

I stared at my father until I could count each tiny red vein in his eyes and the fine parallel lines which began round his firm mouth and disappeared under his close-cut grey hair. There were ten veins, as far as I could see, five in each eye and ten wrinkles. Why did they both come to ten and why had I never noticed before that he looked old and tired and desperate. So desperate that I wanted to spare him any more trouble and to tell him at once that I would never, never marry anyone. My half-brother had run away with a girl whom he had met at a dance and I thought that perhaps my father might be thinking of this and trying to make sure that I did not do anything of the same sort.

I suppose that, had I not been afraid, I should have assured my father that I loved him and would never, if I could possibly help it, do anything to cause him anxiety. But, unfortunately, I lacked courage to speak out. More harm, I thought, is done by what we say than by what we leave unsaid. What we say can and does hurt others, while what we leave unsaid hurts only ourselves. I was punished for my cowardice, for almost at once he went on to enumerate other possible husbands.

The last man he mentioned was Mr Biggar. Against him he brought the accusation that he drank, not in a convivial way or at table, as the polo players did, but secretly in his bedroom. As a proof of what he said, my father told me that he had once occupied a room next to Mr Biggar's in the hotel where he and Mr Costessey lodged and that, after they had all gone to bed, he had heard the pop of a drawn cork. I wanted to say, 'It might have been a medicine bottle,' but I did not, for, in my heart, I knew that the cork of a medicine bottle did not make the same sound as the cork of a wine or spirit bottle and I wondered how it was possible for a man who could write such a beautiful letter on our theory, as Mr Biggar had done, to be a drunk?

Hot blood burnt in my face and ears, so that I was forced to hang my head. In this position, I looked deep down into the polished surface of the table where my own eyes were mirrored. It was through a drumming and a buzzing in my head that I heard my own voice saying, 'No, I will not marry Mr Biggar.' Though I knew I might more truthfully have said, 'No, Mr Biggar will not marry me.' So many thoughts and feelings were revived by his name and so much misery let loose in me by the announcement that he drank that my father had finished before I realised what I had promised.

When we made our way upstairs I was so tired that my mother had pity on me and sent me straight to bed. 'Harry, how could you?' she said reproachfully, but I do not really think she had the least idea of the subject of our conversation.

CHAPTER 19

The Sack

PHILIP AND I were sitting side by side on the hard sofa in the drawing room at Oxford. My head was tucked comfortably into his shoulder and his arm was round me holding me close. I could feel the warm nearness of his body and, although my eyes were closed, the picture of which he and I formed the centre was clear to my mind's eye. A cheap lamp standing on a table shed a circle of light which flared and sank as the cool night air came in at the open door. In this light, our hands, idle on our knees, lay defenceless while, in the surrounding shadows, our heads and shoulders brooded in ambush.

In front of us, on a rocking chair, sat Beattie. She also was in shadow but, as her chair swung regularly to and fro, her knees appeared and disappeared. No artist would, I suppose, have chosen this as a subject but, all the same, to anyone looking in from outside, the picture would have been an arresting one. To such a watcher it might have suggested domestic peace and security but, to us sitting half inside and half outside the bright circle of light, our situation brought no sense of either peace or safety. We had been talking of the future and had only fallen silent when I had become convinced of the hopelessness of a conversation in which only one person is speaking openly. Either because I was tired or because I had a headache, I had suddenly given up all effort to lead my two companions into pleasant pastures of thought and their silence was, if

I needed it, but another proof that they had formed a league to keep me out of their thoughts, their intentions or perhaps their fears.

When I opened my eyes preparatory to making a fresh effort (for their silence worried me), the light hurt them and I was forced to shut them again. And it was in response to my physical and mental discomfort that I embarked brutally on a subject which had been troubling me for days.

'Must a promise always be kept?' I asked.

It was my brother who answered this. 'Go on,' he prompted me, nudging me with the inside of his elbow. He knew perfectly well that I had, as usual, begun with the end of a thought.

'Well,' I explained, 'when one is frightened into making a promise, must it always be kept?'

'Are you speaking of law?' said Philip thoughtfully.

'No, not exactly.'

'Then you mean morally? That is more serious. While in law you have only to satisfy someone else, morally you have to satisfy your own conscience. Can you do that?'

Being at the moment incapable, due to the pain in my head, of thinking consecutively, I let the conversation lapse but, through my lashes, I watched Beattie, who had come to rest when I first spoke, resume her monotonous rocking. I could see her long slim fingers folded on her chair arms and her chin buried in her chest and, to me, she looked obstinate.

'Well,' said Philip presently, 'don't you think that, as you have roused our curiosity, you had best make a clean breast of what has been worrying you?'

'I didn't mean to rouse your curiosity,' I replied, sitting up and brushing the hair out of my eyes, 'but I'll tell you if you like.'

What I said to myself was, 'I'll give them something to think about,' for the pain in my head made me feel vindictive. Ever since my father had talked to me in the dining room at Arcadia, I had been worried by the promises I had made to him. I had repeatedly thought of that evening until I felt incapable, unaided, of facing what future my promises had left me. Perhaps Philip or Beattie might be able to help my tired mind come to some sort of decision. Experience had taught me that they were more practical in their outlook on life than I was and less liable to undertake imaginary responsibilities. I thought, therefore, that they might be able to see round my difficulties and find a solution to them. Slowly and carefully I began my story. Of course I did not tell them the names of all the young men my father had mentioned. It seemed to me enough to say that I could not, at the moment, remember any who had been omitted. That gave the sensation of finality which I wished to convey and, at the same time, spared me the misery of having to be more explicit.

Even while I was describing that evening in the dining room at Arcadia and feeling sorry for myself and as if I wanted to cry, I knew, deep down in my heart, that if my brother and sister were to help me, they must do so without hearing more than the bare outline of the story. I could not complain of my father who had, I felt sure, troubles of his own of which I only knew the fringes. I could ask for help but I could not ask for pity and this, to me, was best summed up in my original question. It, therefore, fell out that I ended my recital as I began it with the query, 'Does that mean that I may never marry any of those people – I mean, am I bound?' Having said this I laid my head back on Philip's shoulder and waited.

At this point there must have been some interchange

of signs between the other two. Maybe Philip winked at Beattie, asking if I were asleep, and she may have winked back to say that I was neither asleep nor dreaming and that he might go on.

In answer to these signals which passed over my head, Philip said slowly, 'As you have told us this, perhaps we had better tell you everything.' And, like the chorus in a Greek play, came Beattie's reply, 'Yes, you tell her.'

'I've had the sack,' said Philip simply.

'The sack?' At this I sat up and pushed Philip away from me. 'But you can't get the sack from your own place!'

'I can,' he replied, 'because it isn't my own place. All the properties belong to Father and Oxford is mortgaged.'

This remark seemed to throw a light on the confusion in my mind and, at the same time, to make clear the cause of our difficulties. 'I know, Herr Bauer did this,' I cried passionately. 'He is at the bottom of everything.'

My brother, released at one and the same moment from my physical nearness and from what had been on his mind, got up and went over to the cupboard in which he kept his pipe and tobacco. With these in his hands, he walked to the open door and stood there, his back to us, his hands busy with his pipe.

'Perhaps that is true,' he said, his voice sounding muffled as if coming to us from a great distance, 'but it doesn't help us. I will have to go at the end of the month.'

'Philip, you can't! Beattie, don't let him,' I burst out, turning instinctively to my sister for support, as I did in every difficulty. But for once she did not come to my aid.

I pressed my hands down onto the uncomfortable sofa and, leaning forward into the light, a new thought stuck me. I turned to address Philip's linen-clad back and long crumpled slacks. 'But what does it matter? We all have our own money. The money which comes from Grandfather William's estate. Can't we use that to pay off the mortgage?'

For a minute or two, neither Beattie nor Philip said anything. They did not seem to be mutually waiting on each other but more as if they were considering what they were about to say and doubtful of the effect their words might have on me. And, when my brother, who was the first to break the silence, took up the thread of the conversation, his voice was very grave. 'We don't have any money.' Then, having filled his pipe, he turned back into the room and going to the desk – the same desk where I had once sought vainly for a place to hide the estates money bag – he put his hand on the baize-covered flap. As I expected, the desk fell open. From a heap of papers, he pulled out a large double sheet and, coming across to me with it in his hand, flung it on my lap. 'Read that,' he said.

I did as he suggested. The document on my knee was a balance sheet and was headed 'William Lewes Estate', William Lewes being our grandfather. It was drawn up by a firm of accountants and signed by Herr Bauer, our trustee and attorney for those properties which had been left us. I did not know much about accounts but I saw that one side of the page, the expenses side, seemed crowded and that the other, which I supposed to be the sales side, seemed empty. There was a large sum on the foot of the page which I did not understand but which made the two columns of figures balance.

'What does it mean?' I asked Philip. 'What is that large sum?'

'Capital,' said Philip brusquely.

'Then the estate is not paying?'

'That's it. As far as I can make out from those accounts,

the estate has been run on capital for years.'

This remark surprised me and I sat silent for a little while. It was difficult for me to understand this apparent waste of capital and yet, being totally ignorant of figures, I could not at once grasp where blame was to be put.

'Why didn't somebody stop him?' I said furiously, meaning Herr Bauer.

'I suppose because no one knew,' Philip replied. 'He is, after all, our attorney and is supposed to be a capable man. And you must remember that this is the first time he has given us any accounts. He is not bound to, you know.'

Philip was staring out into the night. His calmness and his refusal to agree with me roused me to fury – not against him but against Herr Bauer who seemed to be the author of all our difficulties. He had been pressurising my father ever since he had returned from England. Oxford was mortgaged and the property and money our grandfather had left us had been spent while under his control. And who else, I thought, could be responsible for all these things?

'Surely, this involves embezzlement?' I said, going back to my complaint.

'No, you can't say that,' Philip replied.

'Why?'

'Because, although he may have mismanaged our property, you can't say he has misappropriated funds. And besides,' Philip was aggravatingly just and impossibly slow in forming what he had to say. 'And besides,' he went on, 'you must remember that there have been our allowances.'

In spite of the fury against Herr Bauer that I had worked myself into, that remark of Philip's floored me. I immediately began to think of all the things I had bought: my muslin dresses, my Kodak and Coquette. But I could not think that all these things or the things which I knew my brother and sister had bought could have ruined an estate.

'Well, Philip,' I said, 'what are you going to do?'

'Philip won't do anything,' replied Beattie quietly.

'He is going to accept the dismissal.'

'Yes.'

Then, in spite of my headache, in spite of a long training in obedience and a long habit of courtesy and agreement with the expressed wishes of those older than me, I made up my mind to disagree.

'I am not going to let this happen. If you give me the paper and if Beattie will come with me, I'll go to a solicitor in Kingston.'

My sister stood up and shook her full skirts in the lamp light. I had not till that moment realised how still she had been and what control she must have imposed on herself while I had been making up my mind.

'I am glad you think that,' she said, stooping her head until her face came into the light and I could see her big blue eyes bent earnestly on me. 'Because I told Philip that that was the only thing we could do – the Solicitor General would be the best man for us to go to.'

People talk a lot about free will and independent action but it seems to me that there comes a point when, having taken advantage of some freedom of choice, having perhaps under great stress of circumstances made a decision, one is caught up in a succession of events from which there is no escape. Incident follows incident with almost frightening rapidity until, in the end, one is a participator in actions from which one might have recoiled in normal circumstances. As far as our – Philip's, Beattie's and my – personal responsibility for what happened was concerned, I am not yet sure if our decision that night was the original and primary cause of what followed and the start of our independence or if this lay much further back in our lives. Perhaps it had originated in my hatred for Herr Bauer on my first visit to the office or it might have begun further back in the lives of those in charge of our affairs.

All that I know is that, whether responsible through my own actions or driven by something else, I was, on that night, forced into a choice between what appeared to me to be two rights and two wrongs.

It seemed wrong for me to ask for advice outside my family. Therefore, the right thing for me was to sit down and endure the injustices Herr Bauer had prepared, he having become inextricably connected with parental authority. On the other hand, it was wrong for me to allow my brother to be dismissed for no fault of his own when action on my part might prevent this taking place; it was, therefore, right for me to seek advice from a solicitor. Having a headache at the time, my thoughts were neither as clear nor as consecutive as those I have put down. Still the two rights and the two wrongs did then, and still do, stand out. Whichever way I turned, it seemed to me that I was likely to commit a grave wrong and I had to choose one or the other. In the end I followed my affection for my brother.

Beattie's suggestion that we should appeal to the Solicitor General of Jamaica for advice did not end the discussions. It really only began then, for we still had to convince Philip. He was entrenched by habit and repeated obstinately that he could not agree to anything that might drag us two (Beattie and me) into further difficulties and he stuck to his point for a long time. He said also that he could go away: that perhaps, without him, everything would settle down, that Herr Bauer might, when all opposition or cause for bitterness was removed, take a turn for the better. He was determined to look on what he persisted in calling 'the bright side'.

'But Philip,' I said, 'are we to wait and see our estate sold up like Dry Bottom a little while ago?' and my mind ran to the three desperate people I had seen in the Rio Bueno valley.

'The estate is ruined anyhow,' was all he would reply to this.

I, however, knew that we had two strong allies on our side – the side that I tried so hard to think of as the right one. Even though it was dark outside, I knew that Philip, in his mind's eye, must be seeing the yard and the sugar works below the house – his yard and his sugar works on which he had expended so much time and energy. He could not, I knew, wish to give up this well-run estate to some nominee of Herr Bauer's. Then also Philip must realise that Beattie and I, and my father too, would be left in a hopeless position should he go away and leave us. It was this point that I chose to stress when I again took up the argument.

'Philip, you know that Beattie and I will get a copy of the accounts too and without you we won't have a chance.'

'You are right,' Beattie broke in quickly. 'Philip saw them in the office this morning.'

'Well then, aren't we all in the same boat?'

And finally, when he did not reply, I jumped up, ran over to him, laid my head against his arm and whispered, 'Philip, you won't desert us, you won't let us go up to Kingston without you?'

It was this last request which settled the matter and induced Philip to come with us. But, even when that important matter had been arranged and it had been decided that a telegram had to be sent off to the Solicitor General first thing the next morning, he still had something to say to me. Taking me by the shoulders and holding me away from him, he looked down into my face. 'Well, what about your promises?' he said. 'We have got a long way from them.'

'Oh, Philip,' I gasped, 'you mean my promises not to marry?'

A sound in the room behind us made me look round. Beattie was still standing by the lamp, her fair head and full skirt outlined against the light.

'I think one subject at a time is enough,' she said, bending lower to blow out the flame. And in the darkness which followed I could not tell if she was laughing.

CHAPTER 20

Herr Bauer

I MUST CONFESS that the next morning was a disappointment to me. I knew little of anticlimaxes then, except in so far as I had read of them in books. And because of my choice in these, having been mostly of a historical or a philosophical nature which confined themselves to facts or to reasonable deductions from facts and allowed no margin for fancies, I expected that we – my brother, my sister and I – would begin next morning where we had left off the previous evening; and I was very much taken aback when this did not happen.

The books I had read at sixteen maintained a high standard of endeavour. If one chapter concluded in a triumph for the right, the next chapter carried one smoothly along a path of virtuous success. Authors, in those days, left no room for doubt in the minds of their readers. Their characters seemed to know what was expected of them and to do it without hesitation or apparent effort to escape what awaited them.

As soon as I got up the next morning I realised that my brother and sister did not take this view of their personal troubles. Philip was discussing cane-cutting with the head man when I walked out of my bedroom at seven am and, a few minutes later, when he joined me at early tea, he seemed to be engrossed in the estate's management.

His only remark – one he flung at me between mouthfuls of toast, gulps of weak tea, and sniffs at samples of fertiliser

188

which had come the previous day – was, 'Not coming out this morning?' and that, considering I was not dressed for riding, hardly required the polite answer I accorded it. Had he not shouted to Dorcas to keep the post boy as he had a telegram for him to take down to the post office, I might have thought all the misery and uncertainty of the previous evening had never been and that our momentous decision had never been reached. This bawled-out remark of my brother's and Dorcas's echo to it thrown down from the steps to the yard below made me feel as if someone had gripped my heart and hurt me intentionally. I got up and stood hanging on to my chair, watching Philip stuff packets of fertiliser into his pockets and rush to the desk in the drawing room to find a telegraph form or a half sheet of paper on which to write. He was out of the room for a minute or two and, when he came back with the completed form in his hand, I suppose I must have looked incredibly miserable for, in passing, he flipped my nose with the paper. But he said nothing and the next second he was through the room, out of the back door and down the steps calling for his pony.

The form in my brother's hand must, I knew, have been the much discussed message to the Solicitor General and yet he had shown no more feeling regarding it, and hardly as much interest in it, as he had in his packets of evil-smelling fertiliser so little was he apparently affected by the situation. I had during my time in Jamaica been busy becoming what the Americans call 'acquainted' with my brother. The 189 cattle which made up his herd, the pic'ny gang and the cane cutters had been part of a whole and that whole had been my brother. And not only had I been learning to see and to hear and to understand him, I had also been creating a new self of myself for his benefit. If other people had to do this when going through that complicated business of getting to know someone else, I was not sure, but I was sure that my sort of character had to do it and it was not, by any means, an easy or simple business. I suppose it was just because I had taken this whole matter of getting to know him so seriously that, now I did know him and love him and understand him, his views on life should be so important to me.

I wandered out through the drawing room and sat down on the top step of the front flight; from this high perch I could look down, if I liked, and watch the busy workers in the yard and there I should be for some time in shade. As a rule when staying at Oxford I dressed for riding when I got up and remained in my riding clothes until midday, but this morning, feeling that I must mark the day by some outward show, I had taken a fawn muslin dress spotted in green out of my suitcase. This dress was made square at the neck and had puffed sleeves drawn into cuffs below the elbow. It had a tight-fitting bodice and full skirt and, with it, I wore a large straw hat trimmed with green ribbons. Sitting there in the shade, I made up my mind to think over and work out all the problems which had been presented to me during the preceding days. What I actually did was to drift into a disagreeable reverie in which I grew up and refused every young man who proposed to me because I had never been told whether my promise to my father should be kept. Had Philip implied that, in conscience, I was bound to refuse all offers of marriage? To each young man who presented himself to my imagination I replied kindly but firmly, 'No, I cannot marry you. I am sorry, but it is impossible,' adding such a wealth of harrowing detail to their expostulations and to my repeated refusals as left me exhausted. These thoughts were interrupted by a clatter of hoofs and I looked up to see the post boy on his mule come round the corner of the house and proceed down the steep path to the yard. He was a cheerful-looking black boy, dressed in the usual white uniform clothes worn by all outdoor servants connected with a house of any importance. The estate workers mostly wore Osnaberg suits bleached almost white by the sun but patched in squares of varying intensities of blue. This boy, carrying the postbag slung over his shoulder, was barefooted and held the stirrup irons in his toes. He rode in a careless manner and, in passing below, he took off his tweed cap with a flourish. He then drove his heels into his mount's side and, probably to show me how quickly he could perform his errand, proceeded down the hill at a canter amid a clatter of hooves and a rattle of loose stones. Half way down, however, he met the boy with the drinking water coming up the hill and reined in to chat with him. Water was carried in two narrow casks slung on either side of a mule's back and, perched between these, sat Sammy, a bandy-legged black boy.

Although it was still early, the yard was in brilliant sunshine. Indeed the light was so dazzling that it hurt my eyes. Over the garden wall a big clump of scarlet hibiscus protruded and, in the intense light, the hillside burnt as if it were on fire. Against the bleached grass the two figures stood out black on white and ringed in a halo of quivering rays. Scenes sometimes remain in one's memory for no particular reason and this incident was to be, for me, one of those odd permanencies. I was never again to see two people stop to greet each other without a contraction of the heart and a strange sense of loss. Even a newspaper boy stopping to deliver a paper to a pedestrian in a crowded street in London or two old cronies in a village street were to remind me of this meeting of the post boy and the water carrier on the hill at Oxford. And I did not know until later why I was always to remember this unimportant event, which I hardly consciously noticed at the time. I watched the two lads finish their talk while I blinked my eyes in the dazzling light. Then one of them proceeded helter-skelter down the hill and the other came on up towards the house, his barrels squeaking damply against the leather of the mule's harness. As far as I can remember, I was thinking of my brother's odd lack of sympathy that morning and of the determination with which he had shown me just how little he cared that we were about to wire for an appointment with the Solicitor General of Jamaica, a determination so stressed that it somehow rang false. But I suppose that my eyes, detached from my thoughts, registered the picture of the two boys and afterwards reproduced it when reminded of it by any external object. And, for long after the path was empty, I sat staring down the hillside.

Presently I became aware that a buggy and two horses were approaching the yard. Even from that distance, I could see dark sweat on the horses and two little puffs of dust which rose behind the wheels and settled slowly on the canes bordering the road. There was a right of way through Oxford sugar works and, in a minute or two, I should know if this particular vehicle were on its way to Falmouth and the sea or if it were bound for my brother's house. I watched absent-mindedly. Soon the horses turned into the yard and, in another moment, they were breasting the steep hill. So this must be a visitor who was approaching. From my position, I could only see the feet of the driver pressed against the bar and the check dust rug spread over the knees of his passenger. That rug, I knew, could only belong to one person and what could Herr Bauer, its owner, want here when he must know that, at this hour of the morning, my brother would be either in the fields or in the sugar works?

On any other day, I should have jumped up and run away the moment I realised that our attorney was about to call but the last few weeks had altered me. I, therefore, waited where I was until the horses pulled up and Herr Bauer climbed stiffly out of his buggy. Then, catching up my hat, I rose and waited to greet the unwelcome guest.

When we were settled in the drawing room, I waited in silence for Herr Bauer to explain the reason for his early call, quite unconscious of the disadvantage such a proceeding must put him in. He was dressed, as usual, in his yellow trousers and crumpled linen jacket and, in his hands, he carried two large manila envelopes which he presently held out to me. These envelopes, I felt sure, contained Beattie's and my accounts. Had I not expected them I might have taken them when they were offered to me but, being forewarned, I did not do so and retained my initial advantage. My visitor looked surprised. He might reasonably have expected rudeness from me or nervousness, but certainly not this silence and, being annoyed by it, he relapsed into his brusque office manner.

'These are for you and Miss Beattie,' he said, slapping the envelopes down on the table. However I still did not take them from him lying, 'Yes I know,' then lapsing again into silence.

After about a minute had passed in this way, he changed to another subject. He must either have come to the conclusion that my remark meant what it appeared to say and that I already knew of and expected the accounts or else that I was attempting to put him off by pretending that I knew when I really did not. In either case, my knowledge or lack of knowledge could not matter very much or alter the fact that I should soon have to open the envelope and read its contents. So he went on to another matter which to him was more important.

'Do you and Miss Beattie wish to invest some money?' he asked.

'Money?' I said in surprise. 'I didn't know we had any money left.' That rather gave away the fact that I did know and had not been pretending.

'Yes, about £1,000,' he went on, grinning and looking from me to the two envelopes. 'You will find it all in there. Are you willing to invest this money in a mortgage on a good property out here?'

The moment he said this I remembered something Philip had told me a few days before. 'Don't be in a hurry to invest money should Herr Bauer advise it. I heard at the office that he is looking for some fool to take up a second mortgage on a sea property on which he holds the first mortgage.' This had been said before any of us knew about our money difficulties. Philip had not mentioned the name of the property and I, imagining that I should never be asked to invest money, had not thought of enquiring for it and was now sorry that I had not done so.

'Must I decide at once?' I asked.

'Yes,' he replied, with a second's hesitation. 'At once. I came over to see you on this matter and must have it settled before I go back to the office.'

'Why are you in such a hurry?'

'Because I have another client who is anxious to take it up.'

'Oh.'

I have already said that I had carried my hat in with me. I now put it on my head and, tilting it over my face, tied the green ribbons under my chin.

'What is the name of this property?' I asked.

'Thorny Cliff.'

'Is it a seaside property?'

'Well – not exactly.' There was hesitation in this reply and I wondered if Herr Bauer suspected me of having more knowledge than I admitted. 'It lies between here and the sea.'

I could not see his face because of my hat brim and I purposely did not raise my head.

'Is it in good working order?' I asked.

'Yes.'

'Is it well stocked?'

'Yes.'

'How big is it?'

'A thousand acres.'

'Is that all good land or is some of it bush?'

'Good land.'

I called on all I had learnt at Oxford regarding land and its uses. 'It isn't a sugar property? What does it grow – coconuts?'

'No.'

'Fruit?'

'No.'

'Then – what?'

'Guinea grass. It has a large herd of milking cows.'

'Oh. Where do they sell their milk?'

'In Duncans.'

'Who is the manager or owner of the property?'

'Mr Arbuthnot.'

Now I had seen Mr Arbuthnot and had not liked his large fat face, his heavy body or his shifty eyes. I had also heard that Duncans had been short of milk for some time because one or two of the bigger storekeepers had written to ask Philip if he could supply them with milk during the dry months. I was, therefore, on sure ground when I said, 'I suppose it has good ponds but no water?'

'What do you mean?' snapped Herr Bauer.

'I mean that you can thoroughly recommend this property. It is well stocked and well managed?' I said with a show of pleasantness.

'Of course.'

Here I, in my turn, hesitated, trying to make up my mind how much more I dared say without giving away my certainty that our attorney was lying. This property was, undoubtedly, the one my brother had meant. It was not well managed or well stocked. It was, I was sure, dry, and its owner was on the verge of bankruptcy. 'It is,' I said, choosing my words carefully, 'an estate you would confidently recommend to the widow and the orphan?'

Herr Bauer did not answer. I was sure he was staring at me. But I can swear that he cannot have seen my face because my hat brim was still pulled right down over it. Ever since the luncheon party at Arcadia when Colonel Egerton had sat next to me and had read my thoughts, I had been careful to cover my face when I wished to keep my thoughts to myself. Then, just as I began to wonder how long we should sit there in silence, I heard Beattie open her bedroom door and come into the dining room. She must have known that Herr Bauer was with me and have dressed and come to see what was going on. 'Beattie,' I called to her, 'I have had such difficulty in keeping Herr Bauer. He has brought you your accounts and is only waiting to hear what you think of a property he recommends for a mortgage.' I can be sure that I said mortgage and not second mortgage and that there was nothing in my words to upset anyone but my heart was crying out, 'You're a liar,

Herr Bauer. Every word you have said about that estate is a lie and you know it. Where you made the mistake is that you thought we would not know. And what about that first mortgage? I suppose that was not worth mentioning?'

I had a glimpse of our attorney's distorted face as he shrieked out, 'I swear I should have told you!' before he sprang from his seat and rushed madly down the steps to his buggy, into which he climbed and which he drove off, leaving his driver, who was gossiping with Sammy the water carrier, standing open-mouthed on the hill.

Beattie and I stood watching until the last little cloud of dust raised by the disappearing buggy had settled and then she turned to me. 'What have you done?' she asked, looking at me curiously.

'Nothing.' But one does not always need to speak one's thoughts aloud to be understood.

CHAPTER 21

Kingston

T HE POST BOY must have reached the post office at Duncans in fairly good time for, just as we were sitting down to tea that afternoon, a reply came from Mr McPherson, the Solicitor General, to say that he could see us on either of the following days. So, without waiting any further, my brother decided (there being a full moon) that we had better start on our journey to Kingston at ten and drive throughout the night. We and the two thoroughbred horses which were to pull the buggy would, by this means, be spared the heat of the day and should, if all went well, reach the railway terminus at Ewarton (nearly ninety miles away) in time to catch the first train to Kingston.

We ate (or tried to eat) the meal prepared by Dorcas earlier that evening. It consisted of coffee, marrow on toast, yellow yam and Johnnie cakes made of maize meal. These cakes were very dry and stuck in my throat. Altogether, as far as I was concerned, I might have omitted the effort of trying to swallow them but Philip munched steadily and Beattie collected the Johnnie cakes which were left over, buttered them and packed them into a basket which she had brought to the table with her. These, with oranges and star apples, were to be our provisions on the long drive before us.

Outside I could hear the tree frogs tuning up, which was, I knew, a sign of rain. Evidently our long spell of dry weather was about to break and, when I walked out, I looked up and could see the rising moon rushing through the flying clouds.

At the last moment my heart failed me and I longed to be allowed to tell my mother, at least, where we were going. I had never before left home without asking and obtaining permission or thought of seeking advice outside the family circle or even envisaged myself discussing home affairs with anyone except, perhaps, Beattie. Even with Philip, I had never criticised, until the last day, the way in which the estates were run or the way in which our lives were ordered. And this definite action we were about to take seemed to me like a betrayal of something I held dear. Even should my mother try to stop us I must, I thought, tell her where we were going and what we were going to do. Two nights and two days were not a long time, but our object in going to Kingston lent those forty-eight hours an unusual importance. But, when I asked Beattie if we might go round by Arcadia, all she said was, 'No, why?' And, confronted by such a point blank question, I had not the courage to tell her what was on my mind.

So, soon after the big tropical moon had risen, we three climbed into the single buggy which had been brought round to the steps and Philip, like the good driver he was, walked his horses down the steep hill from Oxford Busha House and turned them slowly into the narrow estates road which would in time lead us to the 'Roman Road' which Beattie and I had ridden months ago on our first trip to Mahogany Hall. The main roads were well engineered considering the mountainous country and usually followed the old Spanish bridle paths but, since the trenches which carried off the rain water and ran diagonally across the roads were made on top of and not under the macadam, vehicles dipped into them and came out with a rush. Driving on such roads

could not have been called a comfortable mode of pro-
gression but it was speedy and we were used to it. As I
was the youngest and also the smallest of our party, I was
squeezed in between my brother and sister, 'In case,'
Beattie said, 'I fell asleep' and was jerked out in one of
the thousands of jolts we were bound to meet with on our
way across Jamaica.

From my narrow seat on the buggy I could see the
horses, their manes and tails flying. Where the road ran
under the lea of a hill, it was pitch dark but, out in the
moonlight, I could see the wild country through which we
were travelling. It seemed, for the most part, a desolate
land. After leaving the last village, there were no houses
and no lights, only mountains, rocks and dark patches
which I knew must be bush.

Once up in the hills, however, it was wonderful: rain must
have fallen fairly heavily for fireflies were gleaming in every
gully and the landscape appeared illuminated by a galaxy of
lights. If, I thought, I could hook my carriage to a star,
would my life be any more varied than it had been this last
year? Would I, in the stellar rush through space, see more
or hear more or feel more than I had seen or heard or felt
during these last months in Jamaica? Would I, from infinite
space, comprehend more than I had been able to grasp
during my stay at Arcadia? Or would I drift on, as I now
was drifting, wondering why I had been put on this earth?

The horses harnessed to the buggy were thoroughbred
and well able to last for the long miles we had still to travel.
What I remember most clearly of that drive was the gentle
click and rattle of the horses, the bodies of the horses moving
steadily in the light of the carriage lamps and the dip and
swing of the buggy as it went into and out of the trenches.

We met no one on the road, which followed the contour of

each hill. In and out it went, with cliffs on one side and steep dips on the other, never seeming to progress very far in one direction but always coming out to let us look over a huge valley with a house built on a hill far out on our left. The people in that house were not asleep and it seemed to me hours before we eventually climbed up between the formidable mountains and lost the glimmer of their house lights.

Time passed; I must have dozed for I was awakened to full consciousness to find the horses slowing down and that we were pulling off the road into a valley with a stream running through it. Philip got out and I helped him to unharness the horses and give them their nose bags. Then we sat in a circle and ate the Johnnie cakes we had brought while we examined our surroundings.

The moon was high in the sky, about to drop behind the mountains we had left behind us. Shafts of silver light pierced the upper air but left us, where we sat among maiden hair ferns and little pink begonias, in velvet darkness. We dipped a cup in the stream and drank the cool water. Then, after a time, Philip re-harnessed the horses, put the reins into my hands and told me I could drive until the morning.

If I had thought the first part of our drive beautiful, I found the climb over the mountains which now faced us, and which, I knew, were the backbone of Jamaica, almost frightening. How the early pioneers had managed to engineer that road I could not imagine. Maybe they had followed a native track or maybe they had glimpsed a pass many thousands of feet above the steaming valley in which they had pitched their camp and had made for it undeterred by barriers or difficulties. However, what is well done lasts and the road must have been well done for it had lasted through the years. Up and up it went and up and up went we and our horses and the light buggy. Time and time again we swung round a cliff face high above a wild valley, where cattle grazed in the deep guinea grass, to be faced by a mountain of honeycombed rock. Time and time again, a path dropped from a road to a plantation far below where yams and cocoas were grown. Sometimes Philip motioned to me to ease the horses on a particularly steep gradient and sometimes he looked down over the side of the buggy to a fearsome crevice far below. If you have ever driven through the night you will know how wonderful it is to watch for the first green light in the sky. At eight in the morning, Philip took over the reins and, as the sun rose, he piloted us into a livery stable near the railway terminus. It was already very hot. A huge barrier of hills lay between us and the north side of Jamaica and, in this valley where the railroad ended, there was no breeze.

The first class carriage into which we clambered wearily was covered in dust. The seats were made of slats of wood and the windows were protected against the sun and wind by wooden shutters. Ewarton station platform was already at this hour occupied by crowds of men and women sitting on bundles. Against the barrier, their arms folded comfortably on the top rail, were many who had come to see the train off and to take part in the continuous and noisy conversation which went on between those who were going and those who were staying behind. Philip, Beattie and I were alone in our compartment. When the last package had been thrust in, when the last passenger had shouted a noisy farewell and been induced to enter the train by the perspiring station master and porters, we started with a jerk.

In the gloom of our stuffy carriage Philip took out and re-read the telegram he had received from Mr McPherson. Our appointment with him was for twelve noon. I had not seen Kingston since we had come out from England eight months before and, when we got there two hours later, it struck me as being a hot and dusty place, hotter and dustier even than it had seemed when we had landed and had our first sight of a Jamaican town. The streets were inches deep in an accumulation of dust, the houses were irregular in size and alignment and nearly all looked as if they would have been better off for a coat of paint. After a wash, a brush and breakfast in a big airy hotel with gardens which stretched down to the sea, Philip hired a buggy and took us to Mr McPherson's office.

There it was cool and clean. We were shown into an apartment with windows shadowed in green jalousies and a big desk facing them. We all three remained standing in the middle of the room until Mr McPherson came in and shook hands. He was a tall man with hair going grey and dark eyes which looked sternly at us from behind glasses. I was too shy to notice what he wore but I think he must have been surprised to find us so young, for he said, looking at me, 'Why, you are only children.' Philip, seeing that I had nothing to say to this, answered for me, 'Yes, she is, but I am of age.'

I think that this introduction and the sight of us must have softened Mr McPherson and changed the opinion he had formed of us before he came into the room, for his manner altered and he lost his hard look. He brought forward three cane-seated chairs and made us sit down and then, seating himself behind the big desk, began to question Philip. I listened to their conversation attentively. To me, it was like all men's talk, made up of short sentences which left a great deal to the imagination, but they got on quickly and never strayed from whatever point they happened to be working towards. In no time, I felt that Mr McPherson knew all about our lives, our difficulties and about Herr Bauer. But I only clearly remember one thing he said and that was the following.

When I am feeling shy it is easier for me to take in what I see than what I hear. Things said round me are at times not easy to remember and, when I am more interested in the people who are speaking than in what they are saying, this difficulty is accentuated. I have then to wait until everything is over and I am alone again and at peace before I can realise exactly what has taken place and then, likely as not, I see the past in a series of pictures. This makes the repetition of any long conversation difficult for me. Although I listened to all that my brother and Mr McPherson said, and although I weighed each question as carefully as if it were being addressed to me and each answer as if I were personally responsible for its truth, I did not really take in the whole of the conversation. It was more as if I were examining each card in a pack than playing a hand at whist. My attention did not wander, it just failed to take in. I know I was tired and I suppose I was worried. I could see the room in which we were sitting and I can remember it clearly now. It was high, higher in comparison to its size than any room I had been in before. The walls were whitewashed and the green light thrown by the jalousies cast strange watery patterns on them. Every time a tram passed along the street out-side, these reflections quivered, concentrated above Mr McPherson's desk and finally ran up over his head. For a time I struggled between a wish to be helpful should the others appeal to me and a longing to rest passively and inattentively in this cool, water-like room where facts were being piled one above another into a whole which I could not grasp. Suddenly Mr McPherson startled me into complete consciousness by a question. The only one I really took in.

'I suppose you children do not intend to put anyone in prison?'

I was so surprised by this question and so certain of my own answer to it that I spoke for the first time since I came into the room, 'No,' I said loudly, 'of course not.'

My interruption stopped the conversation. Philip and Beattie turned to look at me and the tall man behind the desk gave a quick glance round which took us all in. 'You are all agreed?' he asked.

'Yes,' said Philip slowly, 'we are all agreed.'

I stared from the two flushed faces to the pale dark one. Mr McPherson might almost, I thought, have been amused, for little laughing lines came out round his eyes and round his mouth and when he spoke, it was as a man who has finally made up his mind. 'Well, in that case, I will take up your case,' he said in a businesslike voice. He assured us that he would immediately take steps to put an end to the position in which we found ourselves.

That was the end of our talk with the Solicitor General.

What he wrote to my father I do not know, but I do know that Herr Bauer was summarily dismissed and that, after my father had been assured of a comfortable income, the management of the estates was put into the hands of a competent and honest man who took over the supervision of the financial side of our affairs.

It might then have been thought that all was well, that good had come out of evil, that all we had to do was to live happily ever after. But things did not fall out exactly like that. My father, confronted for the first time in his life by an authority which he could not gainsay, had a stroke and died and, soon after his funeral, arrangements were made for Mother, Beattie and I to return to England.

CHAPTER 22

Conclusion

HE DAY BEFORE our boxes were due to leave on
their long journey by mule wagon across Jamaica, a
hired buggy, drawn by two tired horses, came trotting
round the corner of the house and stopped by the front
steps of Arcadia. Many such had arrived during the last
weeks, but Mother had not received any of these callers.
She had deputed the task of entertaining and refreshing
all of them to Beattie and me, it being against the laws of
colonial hospitality to refuse admittance to visitors.

Our days in Jamaica being now limited and so much of
our time having already been taken up in this manner, we
had, that morning, begged for one whole day to ourselves.
We had then set to work to take out, sort and fold the
clothes in our wardrobes and chests of drawers preparatory
to packing them into the boxes standing ready in the middle
of the bedroom floor.

After a peep through the closed jalousies to see if this
newcomer could be recognised by his buggy or horses and
finding that this was not possible, the buggy being un-
mistakably a hired one, we had gone back to our work,
hoping to have everything stored away before nightfall and
thinking of nothing but the task in hand.

It was only absent-mindedly that I heard the wheels
leave the front steps and proceed towards the stables. On
any other day I might have put two and two together and
concluded from this that the visitor must have come into

the house, but I was far too engrossed in what I was doing to speculate on what might or might not be going on in any other part of the house. So it was not until someone tapped on Beattie's bedroom door that I paid any particular attention to the buggy and its occupant.

'A gentleman to see Young Misses,' said Albert when I threw the door open to him.

'What gentleman?' I asked crossly, for I must admit that I was annoyed at being interrupted.

'Do'an know Young Misses. Him berry tall gentleman, him know Young Misses. Him stay in de house.'

'Well, tell Mother!' I replied curtly. 'We're busy.'

Indeed this was true. Beattie was leaning across her big double bed folding dresses and I had dropped an armful of shoes when I had gone to the door. Dancing slippers, riding boots, bathing sandals, all sorts of shoes and boots lay scattered around me as I waited impatiently for the house-boy to go.

Albert must have known perfectly well that I was not pleased to see him but he also knew that Jack, his earthly deity, was waiting for him downstairs and that this auto-crat would have a great deal to say should he return without some definite assurance that we were coming to receive our visitor. With a despairing glance at the ceiling and a mute appeal to heaven for assistance, he stepped boldly into the room. 'Me hab tole Big Misses,' he insisted. 'And Big Misses say will Young Misses go and gib de gentleman tea. Him come berry long way.'

From among these stammered pieces of information imparted to me by the anxious boy, my mind seized on two which it grasped and to which it held fast. This visitor was very tall and he had come a long way. Who, I said to myself, is taller than, or even as tall as, Mr Biggar and

who could have come as far? And yet, how could it be
Mr Biggar?

Round me the shoes, lying as they did, multiplied themselves on the polished floor. They were no less tumbled
than my thoughts and yet, in spite of all the confusion in
and around me, the room in which I waited fell silent.

I saw Beattie straighten herself and come across to me.

'Is it Mr Biggar?' she asked Albert.

'Yes, Misses.'

'Then go and get tea.'

Albert disappeared silently and Beattie and I were left
facing each other.

'Hurry up,' she said turning away from me. 'We must go
down.'

But I could not hurry, I was too excited. There can be
no necessity for hurry, I thought, when important things
happen. If they are going to happen, they will happen and
that is all. Possessed by this sort of desperate obstinacy, I
began to pick up the shoes to place them one by one into
the hot, stuffy interior of the cabin trunk. And, having
done this, I went on to collect the clothes scattered all over
the room. A few minutes, or perhaps an eternity, passed in
this way. I had lost my sense of time but Beattie seemed
unperturbed.

The moment she had made sure who this visitor was,
after her first anxious glance at me to see how I was taking
the news, she began methodically to prepare herself to go
downstairs. She tidied her hair, straightened her white
washing dress and retied her black sash. Then, walking to
the door, she threw it wide open. 'Are you coming?' she
asked quietly.

'No,' I said desperately. 'I can't come till I am ready.'

In saying this, I must have meant more than I was able

to express for the shoes and clothes had lost all importance to me and yet, in spite of that, I could not make up my mind to leave them. They were at one and the same time, terribly important and unimportant.

As Beattie neither answered nor moved, I looked up, my face hot and flushed with my exertions, to see what she was doing. She was still standing by the open door waiting for me.

'Are you going to keep him waiting?' she said, when she saw that she had got my attention.

'No.'

'Then come.'

All of a sudden I made up my mind or my mind made itself up without any conscious help on my part. I knew what I must do.

'Yes, I will come!' I cried and, jumping to my feet, I ran to the door and out onto the landing where Beattie overtook and passed me. As I followed my sister down the stairs, a surprising change came over my feelings. An overpowering sense of urgency took possession of me. It ousted all obstinacy and uncertainty from my mind and made me feel as anxious to move quickly as I had, a second before, been loath to stir. And, as I stepped deliberately and consciously from stair to stair, I could have cried with impatience.

When we both reached the hall and shook hands with Mr Biggar who was standing waiting for us, I felt as if I had been following someone interminably and that he had, at last, turned and faced me.

Mr Biggar was, as I remembered him, tall and thin but, in other ways, he had altered. His eyes were no longer vague, no one could have looked more wide awake or more pleased to see us. But he brought with him such a load of my thoughts of him that, for a little while, I was unable to speak.

After our first shy greetings were over, we all three walked up to the verandah where Jack and Albert had carried tea and there we sat down and began to talk. As a matter of fact, when I came to my senses and began to take stock of what was happening around me, I found that it was Beattie only who was talking. Mr Biggar was sitting silent in a rocking chair between us, his long, thin form stretched out to its full extent, his hands on the arms of his chair, his feet crossed in front of him.

Lying thus, he covered the whole width of the verandah and, to reach me with a plate of cakes, Albert had to step over his shoes, the English shoes I remembered so well. And, in doing this, Albert looked so much like a frightened colt faced, for the first time, with a jump that he made me laugh. This tiny episode broke, for me, the constraint and self-consciousness which had followed my previous excitement. And, when I summoned up courage to steal a glance at our guest, I realised that he was no longer terrifying. Each time Beattie spoke he looked at me as if to make sure what I thought before answering. His intention was so kindly, he so obviously wanted to put me at my ease and to assure me that he was no longer cold and distant that I felt ashamed of my lack of confidence in him. Still, undoubtedly, there was something he personally wanted to know.

Then, quite suddenly, I remembered that a little while ago there had been a suggestion that Beattie and I should pay a visit to Alice Reay who lived not far from the hotel in which Mr Biggar and Mr Costessey were staying and that he had, on hearing of this proposed visit, immediately written to me telling me that he had a pony which he would be glad if I would ride. This plan had never come off because, instead of our going to Alice Reay, Beattie and Mother had gone to Mandeville and I had remained at Arcadia with my father during the miserable rainy season. But the remembrance of this kind suggestion was an inspiration to me. Turning to him I said, 'It was very kind of you to say you would let me ride your pony. I am awfully sorry we could not come to Moneague.'

My remark entirely altered Mr Biggar's manner. I must in some way have answered that question which had been puzzling him and in a way satisfactory to him for, almost at once, we were all three talking happily and without any constraint. Perhaps he had wanted to know if, apart from the criticism of our work, we really and truly wanted to be friends with him.

I found myself telling him of all sorts of comical things that had happened to Beattie and me during our stay in Jamaica with the certainty that he would not only be interested but that he would, as a matter of course, sympathise with us.

First, I told him of our ride with the Lockets when we had jumped the dry trenches leading down from the 'Roman Road' near Clark's Town and how my certainty that Victoria could jump had proved true. She had not only jumped but she had done so with such eagerness and anxiety not to be left behind by the Lockets' well-trained horses that I had been nearly unseated by an overhanging branch; and how Beattie's pony, following perseveringly, had done what Victoria had only just missed doing and had left Beattie lying in the thick guinea grass behind her flying hooves. And of how, when I drew up breathless at the end of our gallop, I could think of nothing to say to the Lockets except a few lines of a rhyme my father had been fond of singing to us.

The butcher who killed the ram, sir, was up to the
knees in blood
And the boy who held the pail, sir, was carried away
in the flood.

Beattie, to my excited imagination, had been served in a like manner.

Then Beattie took the lead in the conversation and told Mr Biggar of the horse shows we had gone to. Leaning right forward, her blue eyes sparkling with delight, she described our first appearance in the ring at a local show in a class for ladies' riding horses. For weeks, she said, we had saved up our pocket money and spent it on corn for our ponies. How, on the great day, we had gone to the shady tree, some distance from the ring, where the stable boy was standing with our two entries, to find that he had placed the girths, Jamaica fashion, one round the chest and the other round the belly of our still plump animals. How, horrified, we had unbuckled and readjusted these but that, in spite of all our endeavours, we had been unable to remove all traces of the tight bands from their glossy coats; and that we had ridden into the ring feeling self-conscious and shy.

Beattie roared with laughter at the remembrance of our discomfiture and Mr Biggar joined in. Perhaps, because of this happening and perhaps for other reasons, we had neither of us won the first prize but Catherine instead had carried this off.

'But you won at the next show,' cried Beattie triumphantly.

The remembrance of that second day came back vividly to me. I had then been riding Coquette and not Victoria who had, a little while before, gone back to the pen. It had been a very hot day. I had ridden into the ring in a new white piquet habit with my chestnut mare dancing under me. Quite clearly, I could smell the hot earth again and, in a sort of shimmer of light, see the crowds of black men and women pressed round the ring side. Followed by a subdued murmur, I and my mount had made our way round the oval space, both of us strung up to the tip-top of excitement, Coquette sidling from the human barrier and I, my eyes on the group of judges in the centre, waiting for the signal to trot and then to gallop. And when this, at last, had come and we had changed from a difficult trot into a lovely swinging canter, I shall never forget the cries of 'Coquette! Coquette!' which went up from the packed crowd. It had been like a wave which ran with us and before us, carrying us along on a surge of sound. Later, when I was called up to the middle of the ring and given the red rosette which satisfied the huge gathering that we had indeed won the first prize, one big shout of delight had gone up and my round had been a triumphant one.

These days described had been some of the happiest Beattie and I had spent in Jamaica and, laughing, we shared them with Mr Biggar. And, at last, when Beattie asked shyly, 'Did you think our theory stupid?' he replied, 'Oh no, I have been categorising my friends ever since!'

As we sat on the verandah, one thousand feet up, looking north over the Caribbean Sea, as we had done so many times since our first days at Arcadia, the sun set.

Sunset in Jamaica had frightened me. It did not come gently as in England, but with a hubbub of sound and a sudden flare of colour. The suddenness of it always made me feel that I was about to be caught by some danger which had been lurking all day in the thick trees and bushes and which was now about to spring out and seize me. I had

213

tried to argue with myself and to reason myself out of a fear which had no apparent cause but my efforts had not been successful. And I had finally come to the conclusion that this feeling of mine was natural and that it was perhaps caused by something sinister in the land. On this evening, however, the sunset failed to frighten me. I was able to wait calmly until the darkness swept up and blotted out first the sea and then the land, to be itself finally engulfed in the radiance of the tropical night. And, when the land breeze crept like cool fingers between me and my cotton frock and between me and my silk vest, I, like Mr Biggar, stretched out my feet and spread my hot fingers and was at peace.

To my surprise, I found that I was no longer afraid of leaving Jamaica or of starting a new life in England. Instead of having come to the end of one life, I found I had come to the beginning of another. And that the change from the old to the new had taken place gently like an English sunset and, not as I feared, suddenly like its tropical counterpart. I felt that, when we would drive away from Arcadia in a few days' time, we should carry with us something which would live with us for the rest of our lives.

Northern Ireland. *Front*: Me and Beattie; *back*: Peggy Oram (my niece, Alice's daughter), Mother and Beattie's husband Richmond Noble

Above: Philip in later life on the
front steps of Arcadia

Below: Me in VAD uniform
during World War I

Publisher's Afterword

D IANA LEWES's real name was in fact Nesta Sewell. William (Beattie's son) and Christine Noble were the only members of the family to go to the house sale for Nesta's estate following her death in 1959. Amongst the personal effects which Nesta's long-time companion, Alice Maude, handed over to them were drafts, at least two of them, of Nesta's memoirs. When exactly the memoirs were written is not clear, but from pencil notes written on the back of a 1930s Lloyds bank statement, it appears that as late as the 1930s she was sketching out an alternative ending, in which Bill proposes to her as she is leaving Arcadia – perhaps wishful thinking, and certainly a fantasy that the reader may entertain while reading the work. In fact, in keeping with the promises extracted from her by her draconian father, Nesta never married.

Family history relates that Lord Redesdale (father of the Mitford sisters) proposed to Nesta when she was a young woman and suggested that they elope, and that she considered this seriously but was put off when her family told her that they would never speak to her again. Indeed, Nesta's older sister, Alice, who had eloped with a ship's purser, had already been cut off by her father. During the First World War, Nesta worked for the Voluntary Aid Detachment (VAD) and it was then that she met Alice Maude. For the rest of her life, she and Alice lived together. Nesta was known in the family for her clairvoyance. She was able, in particular, to visualise the whereabouts of pets which had been lost. She died in Yaxham in Norfolk, where she and Alice had lived for many years.

Now that you have read Nesta's memoir, there is one other fact with which we believe a twenty-first-century reader needs to be furnished. What Nesta never mentions in these memoirs is that her grandmother, William's wife, Mary, and the mother of her father Henry, was probably alive at the time and living in the nearby village of Duncans. Perhaps the fact that she was of mixed race was enough to exclude her from the narrative. Or perhaps Henry was estranged from his mother. Or perhaps the mother preferred to live independently outside the straitjacket of a Victorian colonial family. But whatever the reason, Nesta never refers to her grandmother, nor to the fact that her father, and indeed she and her siblings, were all of mixed race. Perhaps this helps to explain why, while acquiescing to much of the colonial status quo, she consistently treats the black Jamaican workers – both domestic and agricultural – with empathy. It might be that this is part and parcel of her independence of mind – an independence that allows her to question the running of the estate and to encourage her siblings to band together to prevent its ruin. For in real life, it was not Herr Bauer, but the very same bullying father, who squeezed the indefensible promises from her not to marry, who was embezzling the family funds. In this light, *A Year in Jamaica* shows the coming of age of a very determined young Victorian woman.

ELAND

61 Exmouth Market, London EC1R 4QL
Email: info@travelbooks.co.uk

Eland was started thirty years ago to revive great travel books that had fallen out of print. Although the list soon diversified into biography and fiction, all the books are chosen for their interest in spirit of place. One of our readers explained that for him reading an Eland is like listening to an experienced anthropologist at the bar – she's let her hair down and is telling all the stories that were just too good to go in to the textbook.

Eland books are for travellers, and for readers who are content to travel in their own minds. They open out our understanding of other cultures, interpret the unknown and reveal different environments, as well as celebrating the humour and occasional horrors of travel. We take immense trouble to select only the most readable books and therefore many readers collect the entire, hundred-volume series.

You will find a very brief description of our books on the following pages. Extracts from each and every one of them can be read on our website, at www.travelbooks.co.uk. If you would like a free copy of our catalogue, email us or send a postcard.

ELAND

A View of the World
NORMAN LEWIS
Collected adventures of a lifelong traveller of genius

An Indian Attachment
SARAH LLOYD
Life and the love of a Sikh temple servant in a remote Indian village

A Pike in the Basement
SIMON LOFTUS
Tales of a hungry traveller: from catfish in Mississippi to fried eggs with chapatis in Pakistan

92 Acharnon Street
JOHN LUCAS
A gritty portrait of Greece as the Greeks would recognise it, seen through the eyes of a poet

Among the Faithful
DAHRIS MARTIN
An American woman living in the holy city of Kairouan, Tunisia in the 1920s

Lords of the Atlas
GAVIN MAXWELL
The rise and fall of Morocco's infamous Glaoua family, 1893–1956

A Reed Shaken by the Wind
GAVIN MAXWELL
Travels among the threatened Marsh Arabs of southern Iraq

A Year in Marrakesh
PETER MAYNE
Back-street life and gossip in Morocco in the 1950s

Sultan in Oman
JAN MORRIS
An historic journey through the still-medieval state of Oman in the 1950s

Hopeful Monsters
NICHOLAS MOSLEY
A passionate love story at the birth of the atomic age

Full Tilt
DERVLA MURPHY
A lone woman bicycles from Ireland to India in 1963

Tibetan Foothold
DERVLA MURPHY
Six months with recent exiles from Tibet in Northern India

The Waiting Land
DERVLA MURPHY
The spell of the ancient civilisation of Nepal

Where the Indus is Young
DERVLA MURPHY
A mother and her six-year-old daughter explore a wintery Baltistan

In Ethiopia with a Mule
DERVLA MURPHY
By mule across the mountains of Abyssinia

Wheels within Wheels
DERVLA MURPHY
The makings of a traveller: a searingly honest autobiography

The Island that Dared
DERVLA MURPHY
Three journeys through the landscape and history of Communist Cuba

The Caravan Moves On
IRFAN ORGA
Life with the nomads of central Turkey

Portrait of a Turkish Family
IRFAN ORGA
The decline of a prosperous Ottoman family in the new Republic

Sweet Waters
HAROLD NICHOLSON
A turn-of-the-century Istanbul thriller

The Undefeated
GEORGE PALOCZI-HORVATH
The confessions of a dedicated, Hungarian communist, tortured by his own regime

Travels into the Interior of Africa
MUNGO PARK
The first – and still the best – European record of west-African exploration